CORNELL STUDIES IN INDUSTRIAL AND LABOR RELATIONS: *VOLUME II*

Cornell Studies in Industrial and Labor Relations are research monographs developed by faculty and staff of the New York State School of Industrial and Labor Relations. Further information about the series and other School publications may be obtained from the office of the Director of Research and Publications, School of Industrial and Labor Relations, Cornell University, Ithaca, New York.

AFL ATTITUDES TOWARD PRODUCTION: 1900–1932

AFL Attitudes toward Production 1900-1932

JEAN TREPP McKELVEY

PROFESSOR, NEW YORK STATE SCHOOL
OF INDUSTRIAL AND LABOR RELATIONS
AT CORNELL UNIVERSITY

GREENWOOD PRESS, PUBLISHERS
WESTPORT, CONNECTICUT

Library of Congress Cataloging in Publication Data

McKelvey, Jean Trepp.
AFL attitudes toward production, 1900-1932.

Reprint of the ed. published by Cornell University, Ithaca, N. Y., which was issued as v. 2 of Cornell studies in industrial and labor relations.
Bibliography: p.
1. American Federation of Labor. 2. Industrial relations--United States--History. I. Title. II. Series: Cornell studies in industrial and labor relations, v. 2.
[HD8055.A5M35 1974] 331.88'32'0973 73-22503
ISBN 0-8371-6375-7

Originally published in 1952 by Cornell University, Ithaca, New York

Reprinted with the permission of the New York State School of Industrial and Labor Relations

Reprinted in 1974 by Greenwood Press, a division of Williamhouse-Regency Inc.

Library of Congress Catalog Card Number 73-22503

ISBN 0-8371-6375-7

Printed in the United States of America

Preface

Perhaps some day the real history of the labor movement may be written, but not now. We are too close to events to get proportions, or to estimate the dynamic power of policies, movements, or men — things are yet too warm from human contact to be estimated coolly and impartially. — Samuel Gompers

MORE than twenty years have elapsed since I chose the subject "Trade Union Interest in Production" for an honors paper at Wellesley College, later expanding it into a doctoral dissertation at Radcliffe College in 1933. At that time considerable public interest was focused on various experiments in union-management co-operation which seemed to promise a veritable revolution in trade union thought and techniques. Reviewing the report of the Committee on Recent Economic Changes (1929), Wesley Mitchell observed:

> Perhaps none of the changes reported here will prove more important in the long run than the changes in the economic theories on which the American Federation of Labor and certain outside unions are acting. That organizations of wage earners should grasp the relations between productivity and wages, and that they should take the initiative in pressing constructive plans for increasing efficiency upon employers, is not wholly without precedent; but the spread of such ideas and the vigor with which they are acted upon by large organizations must startle those who have believed that trade unions are brakes upon economic progress.[1]

[1]Committee on Recent Economic Changes, *Recent Economic Changes in the U.S.* (New York: McGraw-Hill, 1929), Vol. 2, pp. 863–864.

As the introductory quotation from Samuel Gompers[2] warns, however, many of these contemporary judgments proved to be overly optimistic in the light of subsequent developments. The perspective of more recent students, sharpened by their opportunity for observing the fate of some of the much publicized experiments in union-management cooperation, led to a far different evaluation from that offered above and served to confirm the thesis I had originally advanced as to the ephemeral and rather unique character of the principal experiments of the period. At the time I was writing, no published case studies of union-management cooperation had appeared, with the exception of Louis A. Wood's *Union-Management Cooperation on the Railroads.*[3] It was not long, however, before the gap was filled by the appearance of Carter Nyman and Elliot Dunlap Smith's *Union-Management Cooperation in the "Stretch-Out"*[4] (a study of the Naumkeag experiment); Mary Van Kleeck's *Miners and Management*[5] (a discussion of cooperation at the Rocky Mountain Fuel Company); Sumner Slichter's epochal study, *Union Policies and Industrial Management*[6]; and Kurt Braun's *Union-Management Cooperation: Experience in the Clothing Industry.*[7]

On the basis of these studies later writers tended to conclude that a program of union-management cooperation was likely to succeed only under rare and unusual conditions and that the experiments of the 1920's were rather more sporadic than enduring aspects of labor-management relations.[8]

Despite these sobering conclusions the flickering interest in union-management cooperation has never wholly died out. In the late 1930's the Steelworkers began a vigorous campaign of advocating cooperation in an effort to win union security clauses in their

[2]*American Federationist*, Sept. 1912, p. 714.
[3]New Haven: Yale University Press, 1931.
[4]New Haven: Yale University Press, 1934.
[5]New York: Russell Sage Foundation, 1934.
[6]Washington, D.C.: The Brookings Institution, 1941.
[7]Washington, D.C.: The Brookings Institution, 1947.
[8]See, for example, R. A. Lester, *Economics of Labor* (New York: Macmillan, 1941), Chap. 24, and the analysis of union-management cooperation by Joseph Shister in R. A. Lester and J. Shister, *Insights into Labor Issues* (New York: Macmillan, 1948), Chap. 4.

agreements.[9] In the period of the Second World War the Federal Government, through the War Production Board, sponsored the creation of labor-management production committees which, like many of their predecessors, failed to fulfill the high expectations that had accompanied their birth.[10] Since the end of the war, apart from a few attempts to revive interest in production committees,[11] the attention of research workers has shifted to case studies of "good," "constructive," or "peaceful" labor relations, most of which have not involved any formal plans of union-management cooperation.[12]

I have reviewed the main stream of the literature partly to trace the shifting currents of interest in labor relations, but principally to indicate that there is no longer any need to reproduce that part of my original study which dealt with the actual experiments in cooperation. What has not been set forth elsewhere is the history of the change in the attitude of the AFL toward wage theory, scientific management, and production efficiency during the period when the experiments were taking place. This history, which comprised a portion of my study, provides the background against which the drama of union-management cooperation was played out and should aid, I hope, in understanding how the AFL came to adopt official attitudes and policies which seemed so enlightened to some of its contemporaries and so reactionary to others. It may also furnish some perspective for evaluating the significance of contemporary analyses of union-management relationships. Part of my study has already appeared in the *Journal of Political Economy*, April 1933, under the title "Union-Management Cooperation and the Southern Organizing Campaign." The citation of this article

[9]See M. L. Cooke and P. Murray, *Organized Labor and Production* (New York: Harper, 1940) and C. Golden and H. J. Ruttenberg, *The Dynamics of Industrial Democracy* (New York: Harper, 1942).

[10]D. deSchweinitz, *Labor and Management in a Common Enterprise* (Cambridge, Mass.: Harvard University Press, 1949); C. Riegelman, *Labour Management Co-operation in U.S. War Production* (Montreal: International Labour Office, 1948).

[11]See, for example, E. Dale, *Greater Productivity through Labor-Management Co-operation* (New York: American Management Association, 1949).

[12]For a discussion of the difference between "constructive" labor relations and union-management cooperation see F. H. Harbison and R. Dubin, *Patterns of Union-Management Relations* (Chicago: Science Research Associates, 1947), pp. 214–221.

by a number of authors has encouraged me to believe that the publication of the full story may prove equally useful.

The information contained in this study was drawn primarily from trade union documents, such as convention proceedings, periodicals, and pamphlets, and from correspondence and interviews with more than sixty labor leaders, engineers, employers, and editors. A year's observation in the field not only supplied data on the experiments themselves, but contributed greatly to my understanding of the entire movement.

J. T. McKelvey

Ithaca, New York
September 15, 1951

Contents

→ CHAPTER I ←

Early Wage Philosophy of the AFL

ONE of the most interesting developments in American labor history in the decade of the 1920's was the change in the attitude of the American Federation of Labor toward production.[1] Until the First World War, the Federation spokesmen, with Samuel Gompers at their head, were frankly indifferent to problems of production and industrial efficiency, scornful of the productivity theory of wages then popular in academic circles, insistent on the basic lack of harmony between the interests of capital and labor, and unequivocally hostile to the new profession of scientific management.

How sharp a contrast the postwar scene afforded! Instead of inciting labor to militant action, the Federation leaders preached cooperation, reasonableness, and respectability. They proclaimed their eagerness and that of the movement they represented to cooperate with management in increasing efficiency and eliminating industrial waste; they announced their conversion to the productivity principle of wage determination; they stressed the mutuality of interests between capital and labor; and they consulted and associated with scientific managers and engineers.

To what circumstances may we attribute this revolutionary

[1]From the space given in this and subsequent chapters to the official declarations of the AFL, it must not be inferred that all the pronouncements of the Federation accurately reflected the attitudes and policies of individual trade unions. The Federation, to use Gompers' picturesque term, was and is a "rope of sand," its constituents being entirely autonomous. Yet the AFL was the official mouthpiece of the American labor movement at that time; as such, its statements demand consideration.

change in attitude? Had the seeds scattered by the economists at last fallen on fertile ground, or were other factors of environment and labor leadership more responsible? What significance may be attached to mere declarations in favor of union-management co-operation? To what extent were the new ideas embodied in practice? Out of the postwar change such questions arise; their answers will be sought in the chapters following. This and the following chapter will deal with the early ideas of the Federation on wages, productivity, and scientific management.

The early wage philosophy of the Federation[2] might be aptly summarized by the Biblical injunction: "Ask and it shall be given." In fact, until the second decade of the twentieth century, the Federation counseled its member unions to concern themselves only with the distribution of the product of industry. That increased output might also be a source of higher wages was either overlooked or denied. To understand this emphasis upon a program of bargaining militancy, it is necessary to consider the wage theories of organized labor and their relation to union strategy.

Until 1900 the "eight-hour theory" of wages furnished the intellectual driving force behind the AFL. The idea was first clearly expounded by Ira Steward in his pamphlet, *The Eight-Hour Movement: A Reduction of Hours Is an Increase of Wages,* published by the Boston Labor Reform Association in 1865. Stated very simply the underlying chain of reasoning was as follows: Reduced hours would occasion increased leisure. Increased leisure would arouse new desires in the hearts of the working people, who would thereby be impelled to demand higher wages with which to satisfy their new wants. So universal would be the demand for better pay that the employers could not resist, for "resistance would amount to the folly of a 'strike' by Employers themselves against the strongest

[2]It will be apparent from what follows that the ideas of the AFL were very largely the ideas of Samuel Gompers. From 1886 until his death in 1924 Gompers dominated the Federation, stamping it with the die of his own economic philosophy. For this reason I have quoted liberally from his remarks and writings. A competent interpretation of his philosophy may be found in Louis S. Reed, *The Labor Philosophy of Samuel Gompers* (Columbia University Studies in History, Economics and Public Law, No. 327 [New York: Columbia University Press, 1930]).

power in the world, viz., the habits, customs and opinions of the masses." Put more picturesquely:

> The charm of the Eight Hour system is, that it gives time and opportunity for the ragged – the unwashed – the ignorant and ill-mannered, to become *ashamed* of *themselves* and their standing in Society.
>
> One of the first steps in reformation is, to make a man feel as keenly as possible, the meanness of his position or of his behavior. The masses must be made *discontented* with their situation, by furnishing them with the leisure necessary to go about and observe the dress, manners, surroundings, and influence of those whose Wealth furnishes them with leisure.[3]

In a later pamphlet Steward considers the relation of shorter hours to productivity and wages:

> We are sometimes asked, "whether we can accomplish as much in Eight hours as in Ten hours?" To this we reply: "Perhaps not, the first day or even the first year in some cases; though in time, as inventions multiply, we are sure to produce very much more."
>
> But whether we can or cannot is not the question to ask us; it is whether we can *get* as much of what we *do* produce?...Our share of what we produce is the idea.[4]

Such was the mold in which the thought of Samuel Gompers and other early labor leaders was cast.[5] But whether or not they were convinced by the validity of the economic reasoning, it is certain that they found in the eight-hour theory an extremely useful tool for hewing a labor movement out of the rough mass of the unorganized. For workmen had only to organize and secure a reduction of hours, and increased wages would inevitably follow. The

[3]I. Steward, *The Eight-Hour Movement* (Boston: Boston Labor Reform Association, 1865), p. 12. This tract is reprinted in Commons and Andrews, *Documentary History of American Industrial Society* (Cleveland: Arthur H. Clark Company, 1910), Vol. 9, pp. 284–301.

[4]I. Steward, *The Meaning of the Eight-Hour Movement* (1868), pp. 9, 13.

[5]George Gunton and George E. McNeill were also proponents of the philosophy of the eight-hour day. Gompers acknowledged his debt to these men in his autobiography: "I became very well acquainted with George E. McNeill and Ira Stewart [Steward] and familiar with their philosophy of the shorter workday. According to my own understanding, the eight-hour day was a revolutionizing force that altered all the workers' relations both industrial and social and raised standards of living and work" (S. Gompers, *Seventy Years of Life and Labor* [New York: Dutton, 1925], Vol. 1, p. 290).

path to higher wages over the eight-hour bridge looked short indeed and attractive enough to tempt stragglers into the unions. Accordingly the eight-hour day was made the cardinal demand of the labor movement during the last two decades of the nineteenth century.[6] To educate the rank and file in the significance of the standard-of-living theory of wages, an intensive campaign was kept up through mass meetings and a barrage of pamphlet literature;[7] but the basic philosophy was perhaps best driven home by the engaging slogan:

Whether you work by the piece
Or work by the day
Decreasing the hours
Increases the pay.

Obviously such a theory was not calculated to make the union economists overly concerned with the problem of increasing production as a source of higher wages. The idea most frequently advanced and one which could boast a respectable ancestry through Ricardo and his school was that the cost of the new system would fall entirely on profits.[8] A second facet of the theory – the effect of shorter hours on employment – still further revealed this in-

[6]At its first convention in 1886 the AFL requested the national unions to remind their locals that "the primary object is the recognition of the eight-hour system, and that the question of wages is, for the time being, of secondary importance" *(Report of Proceedings of the...Annual Convention of the American Federation of Labor* [hereafter referred to as *Convention Proceedings*], 1886, p. 9). At the 1890 convention Gompers advised concentration on the hours issue: "In the language of that foremost of economic and social thinkers, Ira Steward, 'The way out of the wage system is through higher wages, resultant *only* from shorter hours'" *(Convention Proceedings,* 1890, p. 13 [italics mine]). The strategic importance of the demand was thus indicated by Gompers: "It has been found a most winning and favorable rallying cry to style it the 'eight-hour movement' " (Gompers, "The American Federation of Labor," in G. E. McNeill, *The Labor Movement* [1890], p. 596 g). For an interesting interpretation of the theory see H. R. Mussey, "Eight-Hour Theory in the American Federation of Labor" in *Economic Essays in Honor of John Bates Clark,* ed. J. H. Hollander (New York: Macmillan, 1927), pp. 229–243. The external progress of the movement, which does not concern us here, can be traced in the *Convention Proceedings* or found summarized in any labor history.

[7]Three pamphlets on the eight-hour question were published in 1889 and 60,000 copies distributed among workmen *(Convention Proceedings,* 1889, p. 14). These tracts were *The Eight-Hour Primer* by George E. McNeill, *The Economic and Social Importance of the Eight-Hour Movement* by George Gunton, and *The History and Philosophy of the Eight-Hour Movement* by Lemuel Danyrid. Several pamphlets on the subject were also contributed by Samuel Gompers.

[8]G. E. McNeill, *Eight-Hour Primer,* pp. 17–18.

difference to production. It was argued that the eight-hour day would take up the slack in employment since workers could accomplish less in eight hours than in ten.[9] Yet the question of productivity did not go entirely unnoticed. Danyrid, for instance, had pointed out in 1889 that increased consumption would call forth an increase in production,[10] while in the nineties Gompers and other spokesmen began to justify the shorter workday on the ground that it caused the introduction of new machinery, thereby increasing output.[11] Yet, despite these nods to the exigencies of production, the wage philosophers of the Federation were prone to set no limits to labor's demands. "What does labor want?" asked Gompers rhetorically in a paper read before the International Labor Congress in September 1893. "It wants the earth and the fulness thereof";[12] and McNeill, expressing the same idea more picturesquely, stated the law of the labor movement as:

1. Appetite
2. Hunger
3. More appetite and
4. More hunger.[13]

But after 1900 the theoretical charm of the eight-hour formula began to wane. It had not proved the "open sesame" to emancipation which organized labor had anticipated. The failure of the

[9]The U.S. Industrial Commission of 1898 which gathered testimony on the eight-hour day reported: "The idea that a man will produce as much in 8 hours as in 10 may occasionally be advanced by labor leaders, but it is not their general position; and even if one does advance it he is likely to bring forward in the next paragraph ideas that are entirely inconsistent with it. The argument which really carries weight with them is based on the opposite idea. It is that the reduction of hours will diminish the supply of labor power in the market, and so will raise its price. It will make room for the unemployed, and so will remove the depressing influence of their competition..."(U.S., *Report of the Industrial Commission* [1901], Vol. 17, p. xlvii). See also *Convention Proceedings,* 1889, p. 29, and McNeill, *Primer,* p. 18. Yet, for the opposite and inconsistent point of view that production would be larger with an eight-hour day, see Gompers' testimony before the Industrial Commission, *Report of the Industrial Commission,* Vol. 7, p. 650.

[10]Danyrid, *op. cit.*

[11]For example, Gompers stated before the House Committee on Labor, which was considering an eight-hour law for government employees: "There has never been a reduction in the hours of labor of the working people but it has been followed by the introduction of a new machine, a new tool, and the appliance of a new and swifter propelling force" (*American Federationist,* June 1900, p. 166). See also Schilling, "Less Hours, Increased Production — Greater Progress," *ibid.,* Oct. 1900, pp. 310–311.

[12]S. Gompers, *What Does Labor Want?* (1893), p. 6 (pamphlet).

[13]G. E. McNeill, *The Philosophy of the Labor Movement* (1893), p. 2 (pamphlet).

miners to secure the shorter workday in the nineties had taken the wind out of the eight-hour sails. Moreover, the opposition which organized labor was meeting during the first decade of the twentieth century from the open shop drives of employers' associations, from injunctions, and from trusts, forced it to fling theory to the winds and to place its faith in actual fighting. Though there was less talk about wage theory in these years, the accomplishments of trade unionism were greater than in the preceding period. But all discussion of the wage question was still phrased in terms of distribution and bargaining. Thus in 1903 an editorial in the *American Federationist,* entitled "How to Get More," advised the workers that "wage increases in the past have come from the *power of organized labor.*"[14] In another editorial, replying to a query as to whether there were any limits to trade union demands, President Gompers declared that no limits existed. "There may be, in a scientific sense," he said, "a limit to the upward tendency of wages and the downward tendency of hours, but who can tell authoritatively when that limit is reached.... If we are so wonderfully prosperous and progressive, the workman is entitled to a fair share of our prosperity. Even when he demands more he is within his rights...."[15]

Toward the latter part of 1903, with the inception of industrial depression, there appeared in Federation literature the slogan "No Wage Reductions," which dominated union wage policy during the following years. Just as organized labor's plea for wage increases had been based upon the power of unionism, so its resistance to wage decreases was phrased in terms of ability to withstand capitalist deflation of labor. "It is the height of economic unwisdom," reported President Gompers to the 1903 Federation convention,

to curtail the consuming powers of the masses as a means to industrial revival or prosperity.... The working people should resist any attempt to reduce their wages or to increase their hours of labor. We are better organized and better prepared to resist encroachments upon our condition than ever before; and if perchance some of our efforts may be lost, it is better to resist and lose than not to resist at all, for to complacently accept a reduction in wages is simply to invite its repetition

[14] *American Federationist,* Jan. 1903, pp. 20–22.
[15] *Ibid.,* August 1903, pp. 664–665.

while it enfeebles our ability to resist further efforts in the same direction.[16]

This policy of "No Wage Reductions" figured strongly in succeeding conventions and was dignified as "not only a new economic principle, but a new philosophy."[17] Organized labor's success in averting wage decreases in the panic of 1907 gave a firmer foundation to the determination to resist encroachment upon existing trade union standards.[18] The *American Federationist* jubilantly declared that the economists' theory of supply and demand as determinants of wages had been disproved by the power of organized labor.[19]

In June 1906, an editorial in the *American Federationist* clearly set forth the reasons for organized labor's neglect of production as a source of higher wages. It was an answer to some strictures published by Professor Laughlin on trade union restriction of output.[20] Summoning all the irony at his command, President Gompers began:

...We may say that Professor Laughlin's alternative or substitute for the whole unionist system is what? Nothing more nor less than in-

[16]*Convention Proceedings,* 1903, pp. 15–16. *American Federationist,* Jan. 1904, pp. 40–42; Dec. 1903, pp. 1297–1298.

[17]*Convention Proceedings,* 1906, pp. 19, 117.

[18]*Ibid.,* 1907, pp. 20–21.

[19]As early as 1903 the *American Federationist* had ridiculed "supply and demand." "As a matter of fact," wrote Gompers, "employers have used the phrase when opportunity favored them, and have abandoned or laid it aside in order to justify their charge of unreasonableness now. Wages and labor conditions can be generally maintained by the working people even during periods of so-called industrial depression, providing they will organize and remain organized" (*American Federationist,* Sept. 1903, p. 833).

[20]See J. L. Laughlin, "The Unions Versus Higher Wages,"*Journal of Political Economy,* March 1906, pp. 129–142. The gist of this article was that since unions could not completely monopolize the supply of labor the only road to higher wages was that of increased productivity: "Productivity or efficiency, is a reason for higher wages. To all students of economics this proposition has long been familiar; and why it has not been taken up and adopted by the labor unions is passing strange. Perhaps it reveals better than anything else the unfortunate unwillingness of certain groups of persons to train themselves in economics, and it shows their habit of reading only the literature which supports their preconceived opinions" (p. 138).

Regarding the higher wages which would reward productive efficiency, he remarked naïvely: "It is about as impossible for a laborer who looks out for his own interests to escape being rewarded for growing efficiency, as for a man who is honest to escape the respect of his neighbors" (p. 141). The same idea is expressed in Laughlin's essay, "The Hope for Labor Unions," published in his *Latter-Day Problems* (New York: Scribners, 1909).

creased productivity! Does a workman feel that his pay is insufficient? Instead of demanding an advance, instead of leaving or threatening to leave in case of a refusal, he should increase his output! ... So reason the special pleaders, misnamed political economists of the Laughlin stripe.

According to Gompers, there were several cogent reasons for trade union indifference to output. In the first place, granting that a worker was entitled to wages only up to the total value of his product, it did not follow that he was actually receiving full remuneration for his efforts. There was still a margin for increasing wages through the process of demanding what in fairness belonged to the worker and what had thus far been withheld by the employer. "Does Professor Laughlin maintain," protested Gompers, "that employers pay now, and have at all times paid fair and economically reasonable wages, so that only an increased output could or can enable them to raise wages? That would be too preposterous even for a professor who studies political economy in his library and knows nothing of actual industrial life." In the second place, greater production would not automatically confer higher remuneration on the workers. Unions would still be necessary to enable the employees to demand a share of the increased output. Moreover, in the past, trade union experience with employers who cut piece rates as soon as production increased had taught organized labor that, in general, greater exertion was rewarded by less rather than more compensation. Finally, production did not depend on labor alone, but also on inventions and machinery. Employers might claim that an increase in output was due to improved manufacturing appliances and thus refuse to advance wages. In conclusion President Gompers declared:

We have said enough to show that Professor Laughlin's substitute is of the quack order. It means nothing. It seems simple, but in reality it is a formula which goes to pieces at the slightest attempt at analysis. If the professor had spoken of increased productivity as *one* of the factors of the situation, no one could have taken exception to his statement, but there would have been nothing new or wonderfully original about it, and it would not have affected the question of union policy.[21]

[21] *American Federationist*, June 1906, pp. 390–391.

Even more caustic was Gompers' reply to President Eliot's recommendation that the unions divest themselves of their militant functions and make their "prime business" the fostering of technical training and the encouragement of efficiency on the part of their members.[22] A "union restricted to the Doctor's objects," scoffed Gompers, "would be no more than a sort of debating society and labor bureau, operating under the tutelage of employers, and possessed of nothing more effective than a theoretical advisory function, utterly impotent if displeasing to the 'masters.' " Such a debating society, he continued, might have a place in a utopian world, but in the hard world of reality a labor organization must rely on fighting methods alone. "We declare deliberately," concluded Gompers with his accustomed vigor of adjectival denunciation, "that his plea for the disintegration of a militant trade unionism is astonishingly shallow, platitudinously flat, and shockingly heartless."[23]

Again, in 1913, Samuel Gompers wrote some editorials which showed that, although he was not unacquainted with the productivity theory of wages, he nevertheless regarded distribution as the chief concern of the unions. Thus, in "Passing of the Wages Fund Fallacy" he declared:

> Wage payments are advanced out of capital but are ultimately paid out of the product. That is to say wages are the discounted product of labor. . . . But perhaps the most potent factor of all in raising wage levels is the combined and determined efforts of the workers themselves. This force operating on the distributive side of industry has been most persistently ignored by many theorists. . . . Without introducing any other new factor into the situation, if the employees of an industry paying extremely low wages are organized, wages may by collective action be repeatedly raised. Innumerable permutations and adjustments make this increase possible. That a limit is set to this increase by the marginal productivity of the laborer is generally and historically accurate. . . but added to productive efficiency must be effectiveness in making wage demands.[24]

[22]C. W. Eliot, *The Future of Trades Unionism and Capitalism in a Democracy* (New York: Putnam's, 1910). This volume comprises the Larwill Lectures for 1909, delivered at Kenyon College.

[23]*American Federationist,* Nov. 1910, pp. 962, 970. The rejoinder is entitled "Dr. Eliot's Future Spineless Trade Union."

[24]*Ibid.,* July 1913, p. 527.

It is significant to notice that Gompers had advanced from his assertion ten year previous, that there were no limits to the workers' demands,[25] to the statement that marginal productivity was a limiting factor. Yet, without the perfect competition assumed by Professor J. B. Clark's theory of distribution according to value productivity, trade unions could not, in Gompers' view, trust their fate to the employers but must be militant in demanding their share of the product of industry. "The wage question of today," declared Gompers in answer to Professor Laughlin's declaration that higher real wages could be derived only from a greater output of industry, "is not a question of productiveness but of distribution. The labor of American workmen has been increasingly productive, but the wages of all have not increased in proportion."[26]

Nor were the unionists alone in emphasizing the importance of distribution; they were joined by several eminent economists, prominent among whom were Professor John R. Commons and Professor Simon N. Patten. Thus Professor Commons declared in 1906:

> The success of unions has come about only as they have abandoned the field of production and have confined themselves to distribution. It is with the distribution of wealth that they are necessarily concerned, and the irrepressible conflict of capital and labor is found in the difference between production and distribution.... By painful experiment, or by the experience of others, the unions have generally come to the point of confining their attention to wages – that is, to distribution – leaving to employers the question of production. This may be unfortunate. The resulting policies may seem unreasonable. If so, it is because industrial conditions have separated those interested in the production of wealth from those interested in its distribution. The labor union is a protest on the part of the latter. Its policies are necessarily restrictive.[27]

And later, in 1911, he declared:

> It is sometimes argued that trade unions would be of greater advantage to workingmen if they would make the production of wealth their main object and abandon altogether their restrictive policies. But I

[25] See p. 6, *supra*.
[26] *American Federationist*, August 1913, pp. 618–619.
[27] Commons, "Restrictions by Trade Unions," *Outlook*, Oct. 1906, pp. 470–472.

consider that production is the business of the employer, and that, if a union turns itself mainly to production, it can do so only by becoming its own employer – that is, by becoming a cooperative society.[28]

Similarly, Professor Patten in his *Reconstruction of Economic Theory,* published in 1912, propounded the idea that the distribution of the product of industry depends upon the activity of the forces contending for a share of it. "There is but one social surplus for which all industrial classes contend," he wrote, "and among whom it is divided not in definite funds but in parts altered by each new alignment of economic forces."[29] It was from Patten's remarks that Gompers derived intellectual support for his contention that the interest of trade unionism must be centered in the bargaining process.[30]

While the early wage philosophy of the Federation dismayed the classical economists, it must, I think, be recognized that the bargaining philosophy of wages proved effective in the early days of recruiting the armies of labor. It was perhaps fortunate that the labor leaders were indifferent to productivity theory. For with the rousing call, "The cry of the Toilers is for more,"[31] there was ample hope for making the workers fall into line. But had the slogan been "Work harder, if you want more wages," the enrollment might have been considerably smaller. In counseling the labor movement to abandon its militant techniques and to trust employers to reward workers in proportion to their efficiency, the classical economists were displaying a lamentable ignorance or an astounding naïvety concerning the basic assumption of their own theory – free competition. More realistic union economists knew that such free competition existed only in textbooks, that in the actual workaday world the rewards of increased productivity did not drop like manna from the heavens. Confronted with the demand that they abandon their interest in the distributive process, they quite naturally returned a curt refusal.

[28]Commons, "Organized Labor's Attitude Towards Industrial Efficiency," *American Economic Review,* Sept. 1911, p. 463.

[29]S. Patten, "Reconstruction of Economic Theory," *Annals of the American Academy of Political and Social Science, Supplement,* Nov. 1912, pp. 45–46.

[30]*American Federationist,* July 1913, p. 529. Gompers here quotes Patten directly.

[31]Gompers, *Organized Labor, Its Struggles, Its Enemies and Fool Friends* (1900), p. 6 (pamphlet).

→ CHAPTER II ←

The Conflict between Organized Labor and Scientific Management

TOGETHER with its unwillingness to acknowledge any theoretical responsibility for production, the Federation refused to have any practical dealings with the new profession of scientific management, which was growing up before the First World War. The history of the relations between scientific management and organized labor affords, perhaps, the best indication of a shift in the attitude of organized labor toward production. In analyzing this history three periods are discernible: (1) a period of unmitigated hostility between scientific management and organized labor, lasting from 1911 to 1915; (2) a period of transition during which the harsher features of scientific management were being softened and modified, extending from 1915 to 1917; (3) a period of greater mutual friendliness and understanding between the two, which began in 1919. In this chapter I shall trace the inception and development of scientific management, emphasizing its relations with trade unionism up to 1918. Later I shall describe the period of reconciliation which set in during and after the war.

It was as a foreman of the Midvale Steel Company in the eighties that Frederick Winslow Taylor first conceived the idea of scientific management. His problem, as he understood it, was to secure maximum output from workers, a task upon which he concentrated for the rest of his life, subordinating all factors of industry to the primary necessity of production. At first he employed a system of fines to break up the "systematic soldiering" prevalent among the Midvale workers. For three years the men worked doggedly to resist him; then suddenly they capitulated and ceased restricting output.[1] But victory won through fear made no appeal to Taylor; a less unpleasant driving force was requisite. Casting about for another method of persuasion, he began to analyze the causes of soldiering. These he found to be the ignorance of the employer as to what constituted a fair day's work, group production which was subversive to individual initiative, and the practice of rate cutting by employers. Taylor's first move, therefore, was the determination of the content of a normal day's work by the use of a stop-watch system of calculation. Next he devoted attention to the development of a scheme of remuneration that would afford workers an incentive to reach the scientifically determined standard and that would protect them against incessant reductions in the rates.[2]

The first incentive payment evolved by Taylor and presented to the American Society of Mechanical Engineers in 1895 and to the American Economic Association in 1896 was called the differential piece rate. For a high output, a comparatively large piece rate was paid; as output declined, the piece rate declined. The virtue of this system, according to Taylor, lay in the fact that it penalized the worker for a small output by allowing him less than an ordinary day's wage, while it rewarded him for bringing his production up to the standard set by the management.[3] Moreover, the piece rates were so calculated that maximum production would net the employee fair but not excessive earnings. As Taylor explained, the differential rate "not only pulls the man up from the top but pushes him equally hard from the bottom."[4]

Between 1895 and 1903 Taylor made some additions to his system. He took over from Henry Gantt, another engineer interested in management problems, the task-and-bonus method of payment, according to which the worker who completed a task in the

[1]F. B. Copley, *Frederick Winslow Taylor* (New York: Harper, 1923), Vol. 1, pp. 160–161.

[2]I. Fisher, "Scientific Management Made Clear," *Bulletin of the Taylor Society*, Feb. 1925, p. 43.

[3]Taylor, "A Piece-Rate System," *Economic Studies of the A.E.A.*, 1 (1896), 105–129.

[4]Copley, *op. cit.*, Vol. 1, p. 309.

time set was given a bonus equivalent to 30 to 100 percent of the current wage rate. More important were Taylor's efforts to improve the methods of manufacture through standardization of tools and equipment, routing and scheduling of orders, storeskeeping, instruction cards, and motion study. Finally he emphasized the necessity for a planning department to study the most economical processes of work and to instruct the workers in the efficient accomplishment of their tasks.[5]

From his initial experiments at the Midvale Company, and later at the Bethlehem Steel Company, Taylor evolved a coordinated system of scientific management dignified by certain "principles":

1. Development of a true science of management.
2. Scientific selection of workmen.
3. Their scientific education and development.
4. Intimate friendly cooperation between management and men.[6]

One of Taylor's cardinal theories was that for every operation in manufacturing there is "one best way" of manipulating materials, this way being open to scientific investigation and determination. "Now among the various methods and implements used in each element of each trade," he wrote, "there is always one method and one implement which is quicker and better than any of the rest. And this one best method and implement can only be discovered or developed through a scientific study and analysis of all the methods and implements in use, together with accurate, minute, motion and time study. This involves the gradual substitution of science for rule of thumb throughout the mechanic arts."[7] Because of the possibility of formulating scientific laws of production, it seemed necessary for management to plan in advance all the details of the worker's task, leaving to him the sole responsibility of following instructions.[8]

[5]H. B. Drury, *Scientific Management* (Columbia University Studies in History, Economics and Public Law, Vol. 65 [New York: Columbia University Press, 1915]), pp. 67–86.

[6]Taylor, *Principles of Scientific Management* (2d ed.; New York: Harper, 1923), p. 130.

[7]*Ibid.*, p. 25.

[8]*Ibid.*, p. 38. "All of the planning which under the old system was done by the workman as a result of his personal experience, must of necessity under the new system be done by the management in accordance with the laws of science; because even if the workman was well suited to the development and use of scientific data,

The integral features of scientific management formulated by Taylor were thus the use of time-and-motion study to determine the best way of doing a certain task and the time necessary for its accomplishment, the instruction of the workmen by a planning office as to methods of procedure, and the stimulation of the worker's initiative by some kind of premium payment.[9]

For our purposes, however, the most fundamental question to be considered is this: What place did Taylor leave for organized labor in his scheme of scientific management? To begin with, he accused the unions of being unreservedly hostile to production. "Almost every labor union," he declared, "has made or is contemplating making rules which have for their object curtailing the output of their members."[10] Moreover, he maintained that collective bargaining was incompatible with scientific management. The latter treated each worker as an individual and determined wages in a scientific fashion, thus precluding any kind of bargaining since scientific facts are not amenable to discussion. "Scientific management," he said, "will mean the elimination of almost all causes for dispute and disagreement between them. What constitutes a fair day's work will be a question for scientific investigation instead of a subject to be bargained and higgled over."[11] And elsewhere he affirmed confidently: "I am sure that an establishment running under the principles of scientific management will confer far greater blessings upon the working people than could be brought about through any form of collective bargaining."[12] Taylor thus believed that scientific management would make trade unionism unnecessary so far as its bargaining functions were concerned. He had, however, no objections to a labor movement which should devote itself to educational and welfare work among its

it would be physically impossible for him to work at his machine and at his desk at the same time."

[9]Throughout this discussion I am treating the Taylor System as scientific management proper. It is, of course, well known that the efficiency schemes were developed by such men as H. Gantt and H. Emerson, but Taylor's principles are most generally called to mind when scientific management is mentioned. Moreover, it was the Taylor System to which organized labor was particularly opposed.

[10]Taylor, *Principles*, p. 12. Cf. Amos Tuck School, *Conference on Scientific Management* (New York and London: Harper, 1911), p. 25.

[11]Taylor, *Principles*, pp. 142–143.

[12]Copley, *op. cit.*, Vol. 2, p. 416.

members, and he recommended that the unions look upon scientific management "as the best friend they have. It is doing in the most efficient way every solitary good thing that the labor unions have tried to do for the workman and it has corrected the one bad thing that the unions are doing – curtailment of output."[13]

The unions, however, were not disposed to accept Taylor's counsel and restrict themselves to welfare work, nor were they convinced that scientific management was their best friend. At first no open conflict arose, principally because the plants in which the Taylor System was introduced were unorganized.[14] In 1909 the systematization features of scientific management were installed in the government arsenal at Watertown, Massachusetts, without evoking any protest from the unions. But two years later the union molders in the arsenal struck against the adoption of the premium plan of payment.[15] This strike at Watertown gave the signal for an outburst of wrath from the American Federation of Labor against putative "efficiency" schemes. The *American Federationist* fairly sputtered with invective against Taylorism. Thus in January 1911 the leading editorial, "Machinery to Perfect the Living Machine," displayed President Gompers' scorn for scientific management: "Systematization in getting materials ready for the ultimate workman on the final job is not novel," he wrote, "but scientifically building up the skilled mechanic himself, bodily and mentally, and molding, hammering, filing and polishing him off in order to fit him for his theoretically best usefulness – that charms us unto the very soul."[16]

[13]Drury, *op. cit.*, p. 174, n. 1. Quoted from Taylor's testimony before the House Committee in 1912.

[14]*Ibid.*, pp. 175–176. The few union employees at Midvale and Bethlehem left when the Taylor System was introduced.

[15]Crozier, "Scientific Management in Government Establishments," *Bulletin of the Society to Promote the Science of Management*, Oct. 1915, pp. 1–2. Public attention was also focused on scientific management at this time because of Louis Brandeis' testimony before the Interstate Commerce Commission in 1910 that the railroads could save millions of dollars a year by adopting scientific management. See Brandeis, *Scientific Management and the Railroads* (New York: Engineering Magazine, 1911).

[16]*American Federationist*, Jan. 1911, p. 117. Many of Gompers' objections were based on Taylor's unfortunate assertion that for certain tasks men whose intelligence was akin to that of dumb beasts were best. "Now one of the first requirements for a man who is fit to handle pig iron as a regular occupation," he wrote, "is that he

In the April number of the magazine Gompers made his stand clearer. Quoting one of Frederick Taylor's magazine articles which charged that systematic soldiering was "almost universal in industrial establishments," Gompers emphatically denied the accusation, pointing to the long list of trades in which the prevalence of piece work made soldiering contrary to the worker's own interests. Next he outlined his specific criticisms of scientific management, chief among which were: (1) that it made the worker a mere mechanized adjunct of the process of production, robbing him of all creative interest in his work; and (2) that wages were not advanced commensurately with production. On the first score he wrote: "To the last point of refinement, also, is brought the vice in industry of making every man merely a cog or a nut or a pin in a big machine. . . with no need to employ more than a few mechanical motions, nor any brain power except the little required in making these motions." On the second count Gompers cited Taylor's own statement that the wages of the pig iron handlers, working under a system of scientific management, had been raised from $1.15 to $1.85 a day while their daily output had increased from 12½ to 47 tons. "Will men make of themselves high-speed automatic machines, increasing their output 400% in order to put up their wages 40%?" he queried.[17]

The 1911 convention of the American Federation of Labor listened to a long report by President Gompers on the subject of efficiency. "The year," he began, "has witnessed a discussion on a national scale of the doctrines and practice of 'Scientific Management.' " Organized labor would always be hostile, he went on, to any system which ruined the worker's health and lowered wages

shall be so stupid and so phlegmatic that he more nearly resembles in his mental makeup the ox than any other type" (*Principles of Scientific Management,* p. 59). This kind of crude comparison was also advanced by Taylor in his testimony before the U.S. Industrial Commission. Carefully describing the scientific approach to the problem of determining the proper load for a shovel, he remarked: "We take a proper human animal, just as we would take a proper horse to study. . . . If you wanted to study the hauling of coal, you would not take a pony and study him, but you would take a dray horse, and in the same way you would take a man who is suited to shoveling" (U.S., *Report of Commission on Industrial Relations* [1916], Vol. 1, p. 778).

[17]Gompers, "Miracles of Efficiency," *American Federationist,* April 1911, pp. 273–277.

by substituting unskilled for skilled operatives. The Convention endorsed this report and suggested also that a study be made of the relation between the high productivity of American industry and the high rate of industrial accidents.[18]

In the summer of 1911, in response to a demand from the unions, the House of Representatives authorized an investigation of scientific management with the intent of determining whether the government should prohibit the use of efficiency engineering in its own establishments. The committee, consisting of William Wilson, William Redfield, and John Tilson, held hearings concerning the installation of the Taylor system in the arsenals and secured testimony from employees in the navy yards, efficiency engineers, etc. In its report to the House on March 9, 1912, the committee declared that it did not "deem it advisable nor expedient to make any recommendations for legislation upon the subject at this time."[19] A few days later, however, at the request of organized labor, Representative Pepper introduced a bill to prohibit the use of the stop-watch and premium-bonus systems of compensation in government establishments, a similar bill being introduced into the Senate at the same time.[20] Both bills were killed by delays, but friends of organized labor kept introducing similar measures, until finally in 1915 a rider to an army and navy appropriation bill was passed, forbidding the use of any appropriation to pay a manager employing time-study devices, or to provide bonuses for employees other than as rewards for suggestions about manufacturing economies.[21]

In 1914 a second governmental investigation was set on foot by the United States Commission on Industrial Relations. More clearly than any other single source, the testimony of the prominent

[18] *Convention Proceedings,* 1911, pp. 77–78, 287.

[19] *Ibid.,* 1912, p. 48; Fisher, *op. cit.,* p. 54.

[20] *Convention Proceedings,* 1912, pp. 48–49. In reporting the bill to the Senate, Senator Borah declared: "The terms of this bill and the practices which it is intended to prohibit are directed against the excesses of certain systems of shop management which it is the intention of the War Department and the Navy Department to install in their manufacturing establishments and which we believe to be oppressive to the workmen as they have a tendency to reduce the employee to a mere machine, deprive him of his self reliance, and in the long run would reduce government employees to a condition of unresisting vassalage."

[21] *Convention Proceedings,* 1915, pp. 170–171.

engineers and labor leaders summoned before the commission reveals the sharp hostility and mutual suspicion then characterizing the relations between scientific management and organized labor. In particular the autocratic assumptions of scientific management were laid bare. The engineers were virtually unanimous in holding that collective bargaining of any kind was rendered superfluous by scientific management; not only the task but also the wage was amenable to strictly scientific determination. The idea of winning the workers' consent to scientific management or of permitting a representative of the men to participate in the taking of time studies had plainly never occurred to them. Taylor, for example, when asked if he considered it "wise and expedient to give labor a voice in determining the premiums and prices," replied that he had no objections, but that, since scientific management could be trusted to ensure a fair rate of wages, it was unlikely that labor would request such a voice. Questioned more closely as to whether justice had been "ordinarily maintained in the adjustment of wages," he stated with an assurance which must have shocked some of his labor auditors: "Nine hundred and ninety-nine out of a thousand; it is the thousandth case where it is not maintained. Justice is the universal thing in this world, almost, the injustice is the unusual thing. If it were not so this would be a horrible world to live in."[22]

This indifference, if not positive hostility, to organized labor was likewise revealed by the testimony of Carl G. Barth, a consulting engineer with fifteen years of experience in scientific management:

Mr. *Thompson*. "Then you have not taken into consideration the question of collective bargaining?"

Mr. *Barth*. "No; not very seriously, because I do not shake hands with the devil."[23]

* * *

Commissioner *Weinstock*. "Do you believe that organized labor is a good thing for the laborer and a good thing for society?"

[22]U.S., *Report of Commission on Industrial Relations*, Vol. 1, pp. 789, 798. It must be apparent to all students of economics that whatever the contribution of scientific management to the determination of a fair day's work, the problem of a fair day's wage does not lend itself to stop-watch calculations. For a discussion of this important point, see C. B. Thompson, "The Relation of Scientific Management to the Wage Problem," *J. Pol. Econ.*, July 1913, pp. 630–642.

[23]U.S., *Report of Commission on Industrial Relations*, Vol. 1, p. 888.

Mr. *Barth.* "As I have never been near them, I have not much opinion on that.... You ask me what I think about it, and I will tell you I am too busy to think about it, and expect to be until I die. I did all the thinking I could when I was young, and I don't propose to waste another five minutes in that fashion. I am not going to waste five minutes on the labor-union question until they come to me. If I am called in on something and they say, 'We are unions,' I will say 'What about it? What about it?' We meet, get together, and have a talk with the labor leaders, and I am glad. How it will come out I can not tell you. If they want to be fair and square, I can tell you how it would be. In my opinion, they rank as a set of biased fools that would simply make use of me and waste my time on it...."[24]

That the need for democratic consultation and other methods of securing the workers' participation in task setting was far from being recognized is also shown by the testimony of James M. Dodge, Chairman of the Link Belt Company, one of the first concerns to adopt scientific management:

Commissioner *O'Connell.* "Suppose you make a time study of a man and you set up the conditions under which he operates a lathe, for instance;... you set a time for the turning of those shafts?"

Mr. *Dodge.* "Yes."

Commissioner *O'Connell.* "And after you have agreed with your expert that such and such is the proper time that such work can be done in, and the workman says, 'No, it can not be done in that time,' what is the result?"

Mr. *Dodge.* "We bring a man in there to show him that it can be done."

Commissioner *O'Connell.* "And if he still disagrees with you?..."

Mr. *Dodge.* "If I say two and two is four and a man disagrees with me, and I bring a mathematician or a professor to tell him so, and show him in every way that I can that it is so, and he still disagrees, he is hopeless."[25]

[24]*Ibid.*, p. 896.

[25]*Ibid.*, p. 869. A slightly more liberal point of view was expressed by a few of the engineers. Thus Sanford E. Thompson of Boston declared that, though he had never dealt with unions, he would be willing to allow a labor organization a voice in the selection of the time-study man, but would not permit an engineer representing the unions to work along with the regular expert (pp. 916, 924). Mr. Charles W. Mixter said that he would allow labor a voice in complaining about standards, but would not sanction the use of a check time-study man representing the employees because this would indicate "a suspicion of cheating all the time" (pp. 840–845).

Obviously such imperious remarks were not likely to attract the unions to scientific management.[26] In fact, from the testimony of the labor leaders before the same commission, one gathers that while some of their opposition to scientific management centered about the humiliating aspects of time study – the fear of excessive driving and the dislike of specialization and "robotization"[27] of labor – the greater part of their hostility was rooted in the undemocratic nature of scientific management, in its failure both to provide for union participation in task setting as a means of protecting the workers against exploitation and to admit the legitimacy of collective bargaining over the basic rates of pay.[28] For example, Vice-President Conlon of the Machinists declared that, if any employer with an efficiency system desired to negotiate with the union over the question of collective bargaining, the union would take the matter under consideration, though as yet it would probably not sanction either the stop watch or a bonus.[29] A. J. Berres, Secretary-Treasurer of the Metal Trades Department of the AFL, pointed out that, if the engineers had made any attempt to explain their system to the unions and to win their cooperation, much of the opposition would have melted away.[30]

The technique of such cooperation was outlined by two witnesses before the Commission, Robert G. Valentine, an Industrial Counselor of Boston, and Louis Brandeis, then a Boston lawyer. According to Valentine, the "ideal arrangement" would be to have

[26]Vice-President Conlon of the Machinists declared before the Commission that practically all of the union opposition to scientific management was based upon the "writings and utterances of the authors of these systems" (*ibid.*, p. 883).

[27]The Machinists' objections to the bonus and task system were thus concisely summarized by their Vice-President: "The first is that it requires a task that is always increasing in intensity. The second is that the so-called efficiency systems have been devised solely in the interest of increasing dividends and with but little regard for the employee. Third, because we know that the overhead charge of accounting must be directly borne by the producer. Fourth, that the stimulation held out is deceptive and will disappear entirely as soon as the maximum task is established and standardized.... The employee is not taken into consideration in setting prices.... We believe it is... an attempt to subordinate the mechanical initiative to others, whether they have better methods or not; and the workman is simply an automaton, and loses his mechanical identity" (*ibid.*, p. 874). All the customary union arguments against bonus plans were used in the battle against scientific management.

[28]See J. Frey, *Scientific Management and Organized Labor* (1916), p. 19 (pamphlet).

[29]U. S., *Report of Commission on Industrial Relations,* Vol. 1, p. 887.

[30]*Ibid.*, pp. 899, 910. See the similar testimony of John Golden, President of the Textile Workers, pp. 988, 1014.

three time-study men, one representing the union, another representing the employer, and the third an impartial expert who could act as arbitrator.[31] A similar point of view was expressed by Brandeis, who suggested that the unions be given a voice in the determination of both the proper time necessary to perform the task and the rate of wages, these being problems in which the exercise of judgment played a part. Once these safeguards had been secured, organized labor would find it to its own interest to cooperate with scientific management.[32]

As a result of the conflicting testimony advanced during these hearings, the commission appointed Robert Hoxie, Professor of Political Economy at the University of Chicago, John Frey, Editor of the Molders' Journal, and Valentine to test these claims and to ascertain whether there were any possibilities of bringing scientific management and organized labor into accord.[33] The committee began its work by examining sources of information on scientific management such as Frederick Taylor's books and labor periodicals. It then sent out questionnaires to trade unionists and engineers, visited 35 plants where scientific management was in effect, and held numerous interviews with persons concerned in the movement. On the basis of this carefully authenticated survey, the committee was able to analyze both the trade union objections to scientific management and scientific management's claims in regard to organized labor.[34]

On the whole, the committee's conclusions justified the fears of organized labor regarding scientific management. In the first place, scientific management was not truly scientific in practice. "Far from being the invariable and purely objective matters that they are pictured," read the report, "the methods and results of time study and task setting are, in practice, the special sport of individual judgment and opinion, subject to all the possibilities of diversity, inaccuracy and injustice that arise from human ignorance and prejudice."[35] Moreover, scientific management was essentially auto-

[31] *Ibid.*, p. 857.

[32] *Ibid.*, pp. 991–1011 *passim*. More concretely he suggested that the time-study expert be selected by the union and the firm, p. 993.

[33] Hoxie, *Scientific Management and Organized Labor* (New York: Appleton, 1915), p. 1.

[34] *Ibid.*, pp. 8, 10–11, 15–19.

[35] *Ibid.*, p. 40.

cratic and destructive of unionism and craftsmanship.[36] In conclusion the committee declared that, insofar as scientific management concerned itself with purely technical phases of industry, such as avoiding waste, storeskeeping, and scheduling, it played a beneficial role in production, but so long as it retained its objectionable features it could not hope for acceptance from trade unionism. What was necessary, therefore, was a reorientation of the point of view and method of scientific management to deal with the worker as a human being: "The main demands are for a frank recognition of the trend of events and for some method of putting back into the worker's life the content which he is losing as the result of increased specialization and the abandonment of the old apprentice system. The development of such a method will, of course, take time."[37] On the other hand, the unions should be led to see that scientific management was not wholly black:

> Experience and reason leave no doubt that a close causal relation exists between productive efficiency and possible wages. No one can deny, therefore, that greater productive efficiency and output make possible higher wages in general and better conditions of employment and labor. . . . Insofar as scientific management affords opportunities for lower costs and increased production without adding to the burden of the workers in exhausting effort, long hours or inferior working conditions, it creates the possibilities of very real and substantial benefits to labor and to society.[38]

The report thus ended on a note of hope that some way might

[36]*Ibid.*, pp. 120–212, 133.

[37]*Ibid.*, pp. 135–136.

[38]*Ibid.*, pp, 20–21. From Hoxie's posthumous work, *Trade Unionism in the U. S.* (New York: Appleton, 1924), however, one gathers that Hoxie himself never made up his mind as to whether scientific management and trade unionism were reconcilable or were fundamentally and unalterably opposed. Thus he wrote: "We surely cannot afford to give up the vast possibilities of increased productiveness which scientific management holds out." And he further stated that scientific management "holds out possibilities of substantial benefits to labor." On the other hand, he held that there was an essential incompatibility between the two, trade unionism being static and scientific management dynamic. "Scientific management can function successfully only on the basis of constant and indefinite change of industrial conditions. Trade unionism of the dominant type can function successfully only through the maintenance of a fixed industrial situation and conditions." And later he declared: "Scientific management, properly applied, normally functioning, should it become universal, would spell the doom of effective unionism as it exists today." See pp. 324, 341, 348.

be found to bring organized labor and scientific management together on a common meeting ground, but exactly how this ground could be reached the committee failed to indicate.[39]

Despite the suggestion that a compromise should be effected, organized labor regarded the Hoxie report as a confirmation of its worst fears regarding scientific management and continued to display a hostile front.[40] But while labor's attitude remained unchanged, a movement was begun to liberalize the point of view of the engineering profession toward organized labor. It was the gradual infiltration of emphasis on the human factor in production which finally precipitated a more cordial recognition of unionism by the adherents of scientific management.

To Robert Valentine must go the credit for driving the opening wedge into the block of hostility separating the engineers from the trade unionists. In 1915 Valentine read a paper entitled "Scientific Management and Organized Labor" before the Society to Promote the Science of Management, an organization composed of followers of Frederick Taylor, which later changed its name to the Taylor Society. Valentine's paper fell like a bomb upon the meeting. He began by stating his belief in the worth of scientific management and then went on: "I believe in Trade Unionism as one distinct form of democratic development, despite all its imperfections and its monstrous economical fallacies."[41] Moreover, in line with his testimony before the commission, he declared that in establishing a system of scientific management in a plant where unions existed, he would take the unions into his confidence and win their assent. "If there were some labor union men in this meeting," he said, "I should take pleasure in saying that where I had arranged to deal with the unions. . . I could still get by every single thing that a majority of you people in this room would declare to be scientific

[39]On the basis of this report the commission concluded that "scientific management as a movement is cursed with fakirs," that it thwarted the development of industrial democracy, and that for the most part the experts treated labor as a production problem alone, ignoring "the broader humanitarian and social problems" involved (U. S., *Report of Commission on Industrial Relations,* Vol. 1, pp. 127–143).

[40]See, for example, Frey, "Scientific Management and Labor," *American Federationist,* May 1916, p. 368.

[41]Valentine, "Scientific Management and Organized Labor," *Bulletin of the Society to Promote the Science of Management,* Jan. 1915, p. 3.

management, that I could get by every single element, because the whole business of relationship between employer and employe would have been shifted from the violent method of adjustment to a constitutional basis."[42]

A burst of opposition followed these remarks. Henry Kendall, a business manager, declared that Valentine was a "rank theorist" and that in practice national unions were not given to cooperation. Others stated that if unions relinquished insistence on "equal pay for unequal work" some compromise might be effected. Only Professor Hoxie supported the Valentine proposal, urging that engineers endeavor to understand the union program. "My suggestion to you," he said, "is if you want to promote the science of management, that you change your constitution so as to admit members of unions, and then make a campaign among labor organizations, and if you do that I will furnish you with some names of trade unionists that will join your organization, who are as keen as any of you here, and when you come to the discussion of restriction of output, you will find out why they take that stand."[43]

Although the efforts of Professor Hoxie and Robert Valentine met with no ready response, the issue of consent was not absent from future meetings of the society. Thus in December 1916, Robert B. Wolf, then manager of the Burgess Sulphite Fibre Company of New Hampshire, addressed a discussion meeting on the necessity of utilizing the creative interests of the workers:

The opportunity for self-expression . . . is something that the workman is entitled to, and we employers who feel that management is to become a true science must begin to think less of the science of material things and think more of the science of human relationships. . . . The new efficiency is going to reckon a great deal more with the needs of the individual man — but in order to do this, it must have some philosophical conception of the reason for man's existence. It is beginning to be understood that when we deny to vast numbers of individuals the opportunity to do creative work we are violating a great universal law.[44]

[42] *Ibid.*, p. 6.

[43] *Ibid.*, pp. 6–9. For similar statements made by Valentine to the Taylor Society in his paper "Control and Consent" see the *Bulletins* for November 1915, pp. 3–7, and for December 10, 1915, pp. 11–20. See also his "The Human Element in Production," in *American Journal of Sociology*, Jan. 1917, pp. 477–478.

[44] *Bulletin Taylor Society*, Oct. 1916, p. 6.

And in 1917 he told the same society, in words which have since become classic: "After several years of experience as manager I have come to the conclusion that no matter how skillfully the management determines the one best way to perform an operation, it ceases to be the one best way if the workman does not want to do it that way."[45]

Yet despite these few drops of humane counsel there was little indication in 1917 that a significant change in the relations between scientific management and organized labor was imminent. To the story of this change I shall return later.

[45] *Ibid.*, March 1917, pp. 10–11.

CHAPTER III

Organized Labor and the First World War

THE First World War marked a period of transition in the attitude of American trade unionism toward the problem of production. The need for an uninterrupted flow of goods and services, the participation of union leaders in the formulation and administration of the government's labor policy, the extension of union membership, all impressed upon organized labor the desirability of playing a responsible rather than a passive role in industry. An account of the status of organized labor during the war is therefore essential to an understanding of trade union interest in production.

The Attitude of the AFL toward the War[1]

During 1914 and 1915 Gompers used the *American Federationist* as a vehicle of protest against the war, but in 1916, as America's entry into the conflict grew imminent, he began to talk about the necessity for preparedness. It is probable that, in abandoning his pacifist stand, Gompers was actuated not solely by fervor to make the world safe for democracy but also by desire to augment the power and prestige of organized labor. Realizing that the war would bring production to the foreground of national consciousness, he saw the wisdom of preaching the gospel of cooperation and

[1]See *Labor and the War,* a documentary handbook published by the AFL in Dec. 1918, and Gompers, *American Labor and the War* (New York: Doran, 1919).

service in order to secure public favor for the labor movement. Thus he advised the Executive Council of the AFL in April 1917:

Labor can make this an opportunity for emphasing the tremendous service that it renders to society both in peace and in war, and insisting upon a helpful guiding voice in the determination of affairs that so vitally affect the masses. Labor has an opportunity to render constructive service that will not only have its influence in war situations, but will also affect the standing of wage-earners in time of peace.[2]

In return for this support, however, he demanded that the unions be consulted in the determination of war labor policies. "Now that our nation is giving thought to the problems of preparedness," he wrote in January 1916,

the wage earners present their claim to consultation and participation. No true plan for preparedness can fail to include service for them; therefore they demand that the plans be democratized. . . . The workers are quite willing to bear the full share of their responsibility in any issue. . . but in this day of the workers' realization of their citizenship and sovereignty they are insistent in the demand that they have the fullest opportunity of advice and consent in the council of all the affairs of our nation.[3]

It was not long before a partial answer to this demand was forthcoming. Early in 1917 President Wilson appointed Gompers chairman of the Labor Committee of the Advisory Commission of the Council of National Defense.

Shortly thereafter, on March 12, 1917, Gompers convoked a meeting of 148 representatives of the national unions to draw up an official statement of organized labor's attitude toward the impending war. The document issued, *American Labor's Position in Peace or in War,* demanded the maintenance of trade union standards during the war and the inclusion of trade unionists on war policy boards. "As representatives of the wage earners," it read in part,

we assert that conditions of work and pay in government employment and in all occupations should conform to principles of human welfare and justice. . . . The greatest step that can be made for national defense

[2]*American Federationist,* April 1917, Vol. 24, p. 271.

[3]*Ibid.,* Jan. 1916, p. 49. See also issues of Feb. 1916, p. 109, and March 1916, pp. 177–178.

is not to bind and throttle the organized labor movement, but to afford its greatest scope and opportunity for voluntary effective competition in spirit and in action.... Service in government factories and private establishments, in transportation agencies, all should conform to trade union standards.... Finally, in order to safeguard all the interests of the wage-earners, organized labor should have representation on all agencies determining and administering policies of national defense.[4]

These requests for recognition, maintenance of union standards, and representation on defense agencies were amply met by the government during the years of America's participation in the war, as will appear upon consideration of the policies of various government labor adjustment boards.

With Wilson's appointment of Gompers to the chairmanship of the Labor Committee of the Advisory Commission of the Council of National Defense, the government openly recognized the Federation as the official representative of the wage earners of the country. Thereafter organized labor was assured a place on the various agencies set up to handle the labor problems arising out of the war and a voice in their solution.

On June 19, 1917, the War Department, faced with the necessity for speedy construction of cantonments and camps, signed an agreement with the AFL providing for the establishment of a Cantonment Adjustment Commission representative of the Army, organized labor, and the public. The Commission's function was the adjustment of wages for each cantonment district upon the basis of the union standards prevalent in that locality on June 1, 1917. Later, this agreement was extended to cover all the repair and construction work of the War Department and the land construction jobs of the Navy Department.[5]

At about the same time the Emergency Fleet Corporation established, in conjunction with the Federation, the Shipbuilding Labor Adjustment Board. Composed of representatives of the United States Shipping Board, organized labor, and the public, this agency

[4]*Convention Proceedings,* 1917, pp. 75–78. See also *American Federationist,* April 1917, p. 281.

[5]*Convention Proceedings,* 1917, p. 82. The members of this Commission were E. A. Garlington for the Army, Walter Lippman for the public, and John R. Alpine for labor.

was instructed to settle disputes concerning wages, hours, and conditions of work in shipyards, using the standards existing in the yards on July 15, 1917, as basic and making wage adjustments every six months according to changes in the cost of living.[6] The most constructive decisions of the Shipbuilding Labor Adjustment Board were those ordering the election of shop committees in various shipyards to settle grievances and expedite production. Thus on November 4, 1917, in a decision applying to the Columbia River District, the Board ruled: "The employees in each craft or calling in a shop shall have the right to select three of their number to represent them as members of a shop committee. Each member of this committee shall be chosen by a majority vote through secret ballot in such manner as the employees shall direct. The chairman of each craft committee shall be a member of the joint shop committee."[7]

On October 24, 1917, the Board issued a blanket order for the establishment of shop committees in the shipyards of the Pacific Coast, Atlantic, Gulf, and Great Lakes regions. Although in general the committees proved to be either entirely union or wholly nonunion, most of them were able to improve industrial relations and to stimulate production. In fact, the entire experience of the Shipbuilding Labor Adjustment Board proved "what a great reservoir of latent productive power may be unlocked when all of those participating in industry concentrate their undivided attention upon increased production."[8]

The labor arrangements on the railroads were as important as those in the shipyards. Before the war the trainmen's organizations were strongly entrenched on American railways, but the shopcrafts and maintenance of way employees had had scant success in securing union recognition. Under government operation of the roads, however, the task of unionization became less difficult. In February

[6]*Ibid.*, pp. 83–84. The members of this Board were V. Everett Macy for the public, L. A. Coolidge for the Shipping Board, and A. J. Berres, head of the Metal Trades Dept., AFL, for labor.

[7]A. B. Wolfe, *Works Committees and Joint Industrial Councils* (Philadelphia: U. S. Shipping Board, 1919), p. 116.

[8]W. E. Hotchkiss and H. R. Seager, *History of the Shipbuilding Labor Adjustment Board: 1917–1919* (Bulletin of the Bureau of Labor Statistics, No. 283 [1921]), pp. 68, 97.

1918, Director-General McAdoo issued the following significant order:

> No discrimination will be made in the employment, retention or conditions of employment, of employees because of membership or nonmembership in labor organizations. . . . There must be cooperation, not antagonism; confidence, not suspicion; mutual helpfulness, not grudging performances; just consideration, not arbitrary disregard of each other's rights and feelings; a fine discipline based on mutual respect and sympathy, and an earnest desire to serve the great public faithfully and efficiently. This is the new spirit and purpose that must pervade every part and branch of the railroad service.[9]

An intensive organization campaign followed this declaration. The Brotherhood of Maintenance of Way Employees increased its membership from 30,000 in 1917 to 300,000 in 1920, while the shopcraft unions reaped similar gains.[10]

On May 25, 1918, McAdoo appointed the Board of Railroad Wages and Working Conditions, representing both labor and management, to advise him about labor policies and to investigate alleged inequalities in wages. At the same time three separate joint adjustment boards for the trainmen's brotherhoods, the shopcrafts, and the maintenance of way employees respectively, were set up to adjust controversies and to make agreements concerning hours and wages with the Railroad Administration. Beside the establishment of these boards, provision was made for the election of local shop committees on the railroads to settle grievances — a policy which Louis Wehle has termed "perhaps the most important contribution of the Railroad Administration's labor adjustment system."[11] Still another important development of government policy was the consummation of a national agreement between the Railroad Administration and the Federated Shop Crafts in September

[9]H. D. Wolf, *Railroad Labor Board* (Chicago: University of Chicago Press, 1927), p. 49.

[10]*Ibid.*, p. 58. According to the research director of the Maintenance of Way Employees, the money of new applicants came in so rapidly during these years that wash basins were used to catch it (interview, Feb. 1932).

[11]Wehle, "War Labor Policies and Their Outcome in Peace," *Quarterly Journal of Economics*, Feb. 1919, pp. 332–335. A. O. Wharton, former President of the Machinists' Union, was a member of the Board of Railroad Wages and Working Conditions.

1919, providing for the standardization of working rules, hours, wages, seniority, and apprenticeship.[12]

H. D. Wolf, a careful student of the period of federal railway control, declares that "it would be impossible to overstate the importance of the more liberal rules and improved working conditions that were gained by labor under government operation."[13] For the shopmen and maintenance of way employees in particular, these gains included a vast extension of union membership, abolition of piece work, establishment of overtime rates, recognition of the right of appeal, standardization of wages and working conditions through national union agreements, and union representation on advisory councils.

Another wartime labor arrangement was the erection by the United States Fuel Administration of joint production committees repesenting the United Mine Workers and the companies at many of the mines in the bituminous coal district. The committees were instructed to discuss ways and means of increasing output and "to make clear to each man and boy employed in and about mines that it is his patriotic duty to work the full prescribed hours during six days each week unless prevented by causes beyond his control, and to do his utmost to increase the output." By October 15, 1919, 70 percent of the mines had elected production committees.[14] Joint grievance committees were also set up in several mining districts.[15]

But the result of the separate labor policies adopted by the Army, the Navy, the Shipping Board, the Fuel Administration, and the Railroad Administration was an enormous labor turnover, each agency competing against the others to secure additional workers. By the autumn of 1917 the labor situation was chaotic, punctuated by frequent strikes.[16] The need for a unified government labor policy was apparent. In September the National Industrial Conference Board proposed to the Council of National Defense the

[12]Wolf, *op. cit.*, pp. 39–46.

[13]*Ibid.*, pp. 62–63.

[14]*Monthly Labor Review,* Nov. 1919, pp. 36–38.

[15]Wolfe, *op. cit.*, p. 124.

[16]See G. S. Watkins, *Labor Problems and Labor Administration in the United States during the World War* (University of Illinois Studies in the Social Sciences, Vol. 8, Nos. 3, 4 [Urbana: University of Illinois, 1919]), Chap. 5.

formation of a federal board of arbitration. On January 4, 1918, President Wilson instructed the Secretary of Labor to organize such a board. Accordingly, the War Labor Conference Board was created a few weeks later "to formulate economic principles as the bases of relations between employers and employees."[17] Five members were selected by the American Federation of Labor and five by the National Industrial Conference Board, and each of these groups chose a representative of the public to serve as chairman on alternate days. In its report to Secretary of Labor Wilson, the Board suggested the creation of a National War Labor Board similar in composition to the Conference Board, with the function of mediating and conciliating disputes in industries connected directly or indirectly with the needs of wartime production. Some of the principles by which this new agency was to be governed were set forth in the following terms:

THERE SHOULD BE NO STRIKES OR LOCKOUTS DURING THE WAR

Right to Organize

1. The right of workers to organize in trade unions and to bargain collectively through chosen representatives is recognized and affirmed. This right shall not be denied, abridged, or interfered with by the employers in any manner whatsoever....

2. Employers should not discharge workers for membership in trade unions nor for legitimate trade union activities....

Existing Conditions

In establishments where the union shop exists the same shall continue and the unions standards as to wages, hours of labor and other conditions of employment shall be maintained.

Hours of Labor

The basic eight hour day is recognized as applying in all cases in which existing law requires it. In all other cases the question of hours of labor shall be settled with due regard to governmental necessities and the welfare, health and proper comfort of the workers.

[17] U. S., *National War Labor Board* (Bulletin of Bureau of Labor Statistics, No. 287 [1922]), pp. 9–10.

Maximum Production

The maximum production of all war industries should be maintained and methods of work and operation on the part of employers of workers which operate to delay or limit production, or which have a tendency to artificially increase the cost thereof, should be discouraged.

Custom of Localities

In fixing wages, hours and conditions of labor regard should always be had to the labor standards, wage-scales, and other conditions prevailing in the localities affected.

The Living Wage

1. The right of all workers, including common laborers, to a living wage is hereby declared.

2. In fixing wages, minimum rates of pay shall be established which will insure the subsistence of the worker and his family in health and reasonable comfort.[18]

It seemed, indeed, as though the gods had suddenly showered organized labor with gifts. Recognition, maintenance of union standards, the right to a living wage – all the boons for which trade unions had long been striving were now hastily granted amid the exigencies of wartime production.

On April 8, 1918, President Wilson established the National War Labor Board by proclamation, giving it jurisdiction over all disputes in war industries.[19] The subsequent awards of the War Labor Board affected over 1,100 establishments employing in the aggregate 711,500 persons. Altogether 1,251 cases were submitted to the Board's jurisdiction by one or both parties concerned. In order of importance, the complaints dealt with wages (50 percent of the appeals coming under this head), hours, discrimination against union employees, working conditions, collective bargaining, the eight-hour day, and overtime.[20] The two most far-reaching achievements of the Board were the establishment of some form of bargaining between employers and employed and the promulgation of the principle of the living wage. The Board rendered 226 decisions in favor of collective bargaining, either through the

[18]*Ibid.*, pp. 32–33; also in *Convention Proceedings*, 1918, pp. 60–61.
[19]*National War Labor Board*, p. 13.
[20]*Ibid.*, pp. 19–23.

unions if the plant were organized or through a shop committee if no trade unions existed in the establishment. Some of the awards specified in detail the manner of election and the functions of these committees.[21] Although it never forced an employer to make a contract with a union when no such contract had previously obtained, the Board sustained the employees' right to organize and to wear union insignia and frequently ordered the reinstatement of workers discharged for union activities. The crafts most affected by those decisions were the machinists and tool makers, molders, carpenters and joiners, and street railway employees.[22]

With the cessation of the stimulus for uninterrupted production, the Board was dissolved on August 13, 1919. Summarizing its achievements, the Department of Labor declared: "The board played a large part in the stabilization of industrial relationships to the end that war production was not only maintained but increased to the maximum in the history of the country. Furthermore, it did much to educate employers, employees, and the public in regard to some of the fundamental aspects of industrial relationships."[23]

The outcome of union cooperation with the government, on the one hand, and of government recognition of the right of collective bargaining, on the other, was an immense increase in union power and prestige. The membership of the American Federation of Labor jumped from two and a half million in 1917 to three and a third in 1919 and a year later passed the four million mark.[24] Between 1917 and 1920 the total membership of American trade unions rose from three to five millions.[25] The most spectacular increases were registered by unions in war industries and railway shops — the metal, machinery, and shipbuilding workers. For the

[21]Wehle, *op. cit.*, p. 329. "The shop committee," said Wehle, "was promoted by the War Labor Board at every opportunity as the proper agency for collective bargaining. In some cases the form of this promotion did not go further than the bare finding that the employers must deal with committees of the workmen. In other cases the Board went so far as to prescribe the way in which committees of workers should be selected."

[22]Wolfe, *op. cit.*, pp. 245–247; Wehle, *op. cit.*, p. 329; *National War Labor Board*, p. 24.

[23]*National War Labor Board*, p. 19.

[24]*Convention Proceedings*, 1920, p. 38.

[25]L. Wolman, *The Growth of American Trade Unions, 1880–1923* (New York: National Bureau of Economic Research, 1924), p. 33. See also Barnett, "Present Position of American Trade Unionism," *Am. Econ. Rev. Supplement*, March 1922, pp. 44–55.

decade prior to the war the membership of the unions in this group had remained at about 200,000. By 1920 it had swelled to 800,000. The Machinists gained more than 250,000 new members; the Railway Carmen, 170,000; the Boilermakers, 80,000.[26] The textile organizations also expanded; in 1915 the United Textile Workers had a membership of only 19,000; by 1920 it boasted 104,900.[27]

The heightened prestige of organized labor was as remarkable as its numerical growth. Union leaders played an important part in the determination and administration of government labor policies. The President of the American Federation of Labor was head of the Labor Committee of the Advisory Commission of the Council of National Defense; the President of the United Mine Workers was assistant to the Federal Fuel Administrator; the President of the Building Trades Department was a member of the Emergency Construction Committee of the War Industries Board; an officer of the Granite Cutters' Union was a member of the War Industries Board; and other union officials belonged to the Food Administration, the War Labor Board, and various other labor adjustment agencies.[28]

One effect of this participation of organized labor in the direction of war industries was to endow the union leaders with a sense of confidence and self-importance and to reveal to them the pleasures of cooperation. Gompers, in particular, experienced great exhilaration from his wartime responsibilities, taking pride in his membership on the Advisory Commission of the Council of National Defense and in his directorship of numerous subcommittees. When President Wilson visited the 1917 convention of the AFL to pay a tribute to its President, the veteran labor leader's

[26]Wolman, *op. cit.*, pp. 48–49; 112–113.

[27]*Ibid.*, pp. 110–111. Professor Barnett attributes part of the gains in membership to the government's adoption of the trade union wage rates as the basic rates: "The fact that the trade-union rate had become the government rate, coupled with the additional circumstance that the trade-union possessed an organization for presenting the case of the workers before the governmental boards conferred upon the unions prestige among the unorganized workers. There were other factors in the rapid increase in trade-union membership during the war, but the leveling up of the rates must be accounted a primary one" (Barnett, "American Trade Unionism and the Standardization of Wages during the War," *J. Pol. Econ.*, Oct. 1919, p. 692). The other factors which placed the unions in a strategic position were the rise in the cost of living and the immense shortage of labor during the war.

[28]Wehle, *op. cit.*, pp. 363–364.

cup overflowed with joy.[29] In the late summer of 1918 Gompers traveled abroad as a member of the American Labor mission and was warmly greeted by the royal and parliamentary dignitaries of Europe. Thus to be praised by eminent statesmen and by the President of the United States and to be complimented by industrial leaders was a novel and pleasurable experience in Gompers' battle-scarred career. He says quite frankly in his autobiography: "To me the War had been a crusade inspired by concern for the higher welfare of humanity and glorifying the spirit of service. I had flung myself into the cause without reservation, happy to find myself in harmony with so many. All my life has been a fight and it has so often been my duty to say that which but few wanted to hear."[30]

A second effect of the leaders' share in the management of war industries was to initiate them into the problems of production, to tinge them slightly with the point of view of industrial managers, and, by bringing them into contact with technical experts, to soften their previous hostility to "intellectuals"[31] and efficiency engineers. As Selig Perlman points out:

America's entry into the war opened to many intellectuals a never-to be-forgotten place in industry — as the "President's investigators," as members of policy-forming boards, as industrial conciliators and arbitrators, as personnel directors and advisors and so forth. . . . Also the labor organizations now became alive to the need for the services of intellectuals who were economic and statistical experts as spokesmen before the numerous government boards with powers over labor conditions.[32]

Contact with the profession of scientific management was furnished primarily by Gompers' association with Morris L. Cooke, a promi-

[29]Gompers, *Seventy Years of Life and Labor,* Vol. 2, p. 385.

[30]*Ibid.,* p. 513.

[31]According to Commons' definition, the term "intellectual" may be applied to any person whose own "economic interest or means of livelihood lies, for the time being, in any direction other than that of wages derived from their own manual work" (Commons, *History of Labor in the United States* [New York: Macmillan, 1921], Vol. 1, p. 19). For an excellent account of the prewar attitude of organized labor toward the "intellectuals" see L. W. Cooper, "A. F. of L. and the Intellectuals," *Political Science Quarterly,* Sept. 1928, pp. 388–394.

[32]S. Perlman, *A Theory of the Labor Movement* (New York: Macmillan, 1928), p. 181.

nent industrial engineer who served on various government boards and commissions during the war. Mr. Cooke brought to Gompers' attention the hitherto unsuspected sabotage and industrial wastes which the war had revealed.[33] In the years following the war, as we shall have occasion to note later, the unions began to avail themselves of the technical services which the war had taught them to appreciate.

Thus the emphasis of the war on production, the growth in union power and prestige resultant from labor's cooperation with the government, the association of labor leaders with industrial managers and "intellectuals," all imbued the labor movement with a new sense of responsibility, self-confidence, and assurance and vividly demonstrated that the gains which militancy had been unable to secure might be won through a program of consultation and cooperation. This new sense of power and responsibility was revealed in the reconstruction program of the AFL.

The Reconstruction Proposals of the American Federation of Labor

During the war the American Federation of Labor was constantly advancing suggestions for the conduct of industry in time of peace. With their emphasis upon cooperation and industrial democracy, these proposals constitute the first official indication of trade union interest in production and problems of shop management. Shaped, for the most part, by the wartime experiences of the American labor movement described in the preceding pages, these proposals were also somewhat influenced by certain English projects for industrial reconstruction.

In 1916 the Garton Foundation of England privately circulated among employers, trade unionists, and public men of all parties a *Memorandum on the Industrial Situation after the War,* which was later reprinted and distributed in the United States by the Shipbuilding Labor Adjustment Board. This document declared that production must be the focal point of industrial endeavor after the war, that to secure efficient production labor, capital, and management must cooperate, and that labor must no longer be

[33]Interview with Mr. Cooke, Dec. 16, 1931, and with Miss Thorne, Jan. 14, 1932.

treated as a commodity and brainless automaton but must be accorded a responsible status in industry.

The Foundation suggested that joint committees representing labor and management be set up in each establishment to discuss problems of efficiency and that joint national councils be created in each industry to consider quantity and quality of output, research, apprentice training, prevention of unemployment, and systems of wage payment. In organized industries it was proposed to have the unions represent the workers.[34]

As a result of these suggestions for reconstruction the Minister of Labour appointed the Right Hon. J. H. Whitley, M. P., head of a committee to consider plans "for securing a permanent improvement in the relations between employers and workmen and to recommend means for securing that industrial conditions affecting the relations between employers and workmen shall be systematically reviewed by those concerned with a view to improving conditions in the future."[35] In its first report, rendered March 8, 1917, and dealing with industries in which both employers and employees were organized, the Whitley Committee recommended that after the war the cooperation of all parties in industry should continue. To the end that permanent improvement in industrial relations might be effected, the Committee proposed the establishment in each industry of a hierarchy of joint works, district, and national councils, representing the trade unions and the employers' associations to discuss such matters as the following:

1. The better utilization of the practical knowledge and experience of the workpeople.
2. Means for securing to the workpeople a greater share in and responsibility for the determination and observation of the conditions under which their work is carried on.
3. The settlement of the general principles governing the conditions of employment.
4. Technical education and training.
5. Industrial research and the full utilization of its results.
6. The provision of facilities for the full consideration and utiliza-

[34]Carton Foundation, *Memorandum on the Industrial Situation after the War* (London: Harrison, 1916), pp. 71–72, 81–84.

[35]Bureau of Industrial Research, *The Industrial Council Plan in Great Britain* (1919), p. 12.

tion of inventions and improvements designed by workpeople, and for the adequate safeguarding of the rights of the designers of such improvements.

7. Improvements of processes, machinery and organization and appropriate questions relating to the management and examination of industrial experiments with special reference to cooperation in carrying new ideas into effect and full consideration of the workpeople's point of view in relation to them.[36]

In its second report on October 18, 1917, the Committee dealt with the machinery of cooperation for semiorganized and unorganized industries.[37] The third report, also issued on October 18, 1917, summarized the preceding documents and emphasized the necessity for the joint councils to confine their attention to production, leaving hours and wages to be settled by district and national agreements. The success of the councils, said the Committee, would be promoted by organization of the employers and the employees: "It is strongly felt that the setting up of works committees without the cooperation of the trade unions and the employers' associations in the trade or branch of trade concerned would stand in the way of improved industrial relationships which in these reports we are endeavoring to further."[38]

The Garton and Whitley reports undoubtedly exerted a profound influence upon the thought of the American Federation of Labor, for they were quoted frequently and favorably both in the conventions of the Federation and in the pages of the *American Federationist* and were incorporated in the Federation's own reconstruction program.[39] In 1917 the Executive Council reported to the Federation convention that out of the struggle for political democracy was being born a new conception of industrial democracy in which the workers would be accorded a voice in the management of industry. Adverting to the Whitley platform, the Council stressed the necessity for postwar cooperation between capital and labor through some form of joint organization.[40] Again, in

[36]*Ibid.*, pp. 16–17.
[37]*Ibid.*, pp. 30–31.
[38]*Ibid.*, p. 36.
[39]See, for example, *American Federationist*, Oct. 1917, p. 855.
[40]*Convention Proceedings*, 1917, pp. 137–138. See also *American Federationist*, Nov. 1917, pp. 989–990.

1918 the Executive Council outlined organized labor's "constructive demands" for cooperation and union participation in management after the war. "Betterment for wage earners under all circumstances," read the report, "depends upon the control they exercise through economic organization. Control brings with it responsibility. The right of workers to a share in the results of increasing production... means greater interest in increasing output." Then followed a remarkable declaration in favor of shop committees, approval which the Federation was soon to rescind after bitter experience with company unions:

> The Executive Council believes that in all large permanent shops a regular arrangement should be provided whereby:
>
> *First,* a committee of the workers would regularly meet with the shop management to confer over matters of production; and whereby:
>
> *Second,* such committee could carry, beyond the foreman and the superintendent to the general manager or to the president, any important grievance which the workers may have with reference to wages, hours and conditions.
>
> It is fundamental for efficiency in production that the essentials of team work be understood and followed by all. There must be opportunity for intercourse and exchange of viewpoints between workers and managers. It is the machinery for solving industrial problems that is fundamental.[41]

In December 1918 the *American Federationist* contained the following hopeful prognosis:

> The world is entering the period of its remaking.... We shall do well to look upon this remaking, not as a rebuilding of what we had before

[41] *Convention Proceedings,* 1918, p. 85. Referring to this declaration Gompers spoke approvingly of the shop committee which had been established in the Bethlehem Steel Company by order of the War Labor Board: "The same benefits may be established for the workers in every other place where a shop-committee is inaugurated; nor is it necessary to wait for an award from the War Labor Board. Shop committees can be established through the initiative of the workers themselves.... The best developments for war production ought to be utilized for the perfection of our permanent industrial structure" *(American Federationist,* Sept. 1918, p. 811). This editorial, entitled "Labor Representation Essential," discusses in detailed fashion the report of the British Ministry of Labour on Works Committees. It is interesting to observe that the Federation saw at this time no threat to trade unionism in the shop committee. The leaders apparently believed that in the unionized plants the shop committee would be controlled by the organization, while in the nonunion establishments a plan of employee representation would serve as an opening wedge to union recognition.

1914, but as a creating of something far better than that. We must not forget the lesson that the great war has taught us.... Precedent has lost much of its unhappy charm. We look more to the present fact and the future need than to the lasting range of what has been done in the past.... Labor made definite constructive proposals for war. It has definite constructive proposals for peace — for human life and standards and relations in peace.... Labor is going to be consistently FOR DEMOCRACY.[42]

The end of the war thus found the American Federation of Labor looking forward expectantly to an era of peace and democracy in industry. From its own wartime experiences and from the British reconstruction proposals, organized labor derived assurance that mutual cooperation and consultation would be the pillars of the new industrial order.[43]

[42] *American Federationist,* Dec. 1918, pp. 1089–1093 *passim.* Much of this talk about "industrial democracy" was exceedingly vague — as are most formulations of an ideal. At the time it is doubtful whether the labor spokesmen had in mind anything more than a further extension and intensification of collective bargaining. For example, Matthew Woll wrote in 1919: "It is through collective action and by collective bargaining that the American wage-earners intend to establish industrial democracy.... What the American workers conceive as industrial democracy is the freedom to associate, and by voluntary collective action express their demands and wants, present them to the employers for agreement and appeal to the general public for its encouragement and support" ("Organized Labor and Democracy," *Publications of the American Sociological Society,* Dec. 1919, p. 57).

[43] That the wartime experiences marked the beginning of a new era in industrial relations was likewise the opinion of many contemporary observers. For example, Professor Watkins declared in 1919: "If the war has resulted in any constructive effect upon industrial society it has certainly demonstrated the possibility and practicability of harmonious relations and earnest cooperation between the parties to industry — capital, management, labor and the government.... [The] intimate association of the representatives of management and capital with the representatives of labor has done much to modify the harsh opinion each group of interests has held concerning the other, and should contribute materially to the elimination of the antagonism that has characterized modern industrial relations and disrupted industrial peace" (Watkins, *op. cit.,* pp. 225–226).

Similarly Professor A. B. Wolfe observed in 1919: "Labor and capital have buried the hatchet — not deep perhaps, but still buried — and put their shoulders to the wheel of production. There are indications that labor and capital understand each other better than they did two years ago, and both sides show a tendency to grasp the fact that cooperation and a square deal will accomplish both a greater output and more justice than will antagonism and conflict" (Wolfe, *op. cit.,* p. 142).

→ CHAPTER IV ←

The Industrial Environment of Trade Unionism in the Twenties

UNFORTUNATELY, labor's roseate expectations of a new era of industrial democracy that was to rise from the ashes of the war were soon to be dashed to the ground. For a short time after the armistice the unions were able to make their newly acquired power felt, but increasing signs of industrial instability brought a renewal of the old hostility between labor and management. From the public, from employers, from the courts there came a mounting chorus of opposition to unions, threatening not only the gains acquired during the war but also those won prior to 1917.

Yet this was the decade in which trade union interest in production, first faintly expressed during the prosperous years of wartime recognition, grew with astonishing rapidity, the decade in which the AFL boasted of its acquaintance with scientific managers and efficiency engineers and talked long and loud of union-management cooperation and the significance of increased output as a source of higher wages. This, moreover, was the period which witnessed the first outcropping of specific experiments in union-management cooperation either through joint shop committees to consider matters of productive efficiency and the elimination of waste or through union engineering and union participation in job analysis and the setting of standards of production.

This significant trend was more directly related to the changing climate of opinion than might at first appear. Therefore, before examining these new developments in the field of union policy, it will be helpful to review briefly the main factors in the industrial background of the decade in order to discover their possible bearing on the growth of trade union interest in production. We shall be concerned more particularly with those features of the decade which made the task of organized labor either more difficult than in former years or different.

Having grown steadily during the war, public regard for organized labor diminished strikingly in the years following the armistice. There was a widespread belief that the trade unions were not only restricting output but also harboring revolutionary designs. In considering this revived hostility and labor's reaction thereto, it must constantly be remembered that Gompers had always emphasized the importance of a favorable public attitude toward the unions. His participation in the National Civic Federation as early as the first decade of the twentieth century was actuated by a desire to commend the unions to the public. "To have the support of public opinion," he wrote in his autobiography, "was of strategic advantage in arguing for recognition as a normal industrial agency."[1]

Hence, when the charge that labor organizations were curtailing output began to gain circulation after the war, Gompers was seriously worried. The accusation was featured prominently in periodicals and economic discussions. For example, Waddill Catchings declared in the *Atlantic Monthly* for February 1922: "The labor union seeks to get more for the workman and to make it possible for him to work less. Whatever the workman gets, the labor union is interested in seeing him get more; however little he may work, it is better if he works less."[2] It is true that organized labor had always been charged with restricting output, but the post-war indictment, based on the soaring cost of living, on the need for production to replace the wastage of the war, and on the Lock-

[1]Gompers, *Seventy Years of Life and Labor,* Vol. 2, p. 105.

[2]Catchings, "Our Common Enterprise," *Atlantic Monthly,* Feb. 1922, p. 219. See also C. Noyes, "The Economics of Trade-Unionism," *North American Review,* Jan. 1921, pp. 16–24. For Gompers' comment on this article see *American Federationist,* Feb. 1921, pp. 142–146. Reference should also be made to M. B. Hammond's remarks before the American Economic Association, *Am. Econ. Rev. Supp.,* March 1922, pp. 86–87.

wood Committee's disclosure of flagrant union restrictions in the New York building trades, was particularly severe. Again and again in the pages of the *American Federationist* Gompers denied the arraignment and asserted that unionism was fundamentally concerned with increasing production. The blame for restricted output rested squarely on the shoulders of employers who were purposely refraining from utilizing the full production capacities of their plants in order to raise prices. "Labor," declared Gompers in 1919, "demands a real relief from profiteering. It understands thoroughly the necessity for production, being engaged constantly in doing the useful and essential work of the world."[3] A year later, adverting to the dismissal of 12,000 employees by the Pennsylvania Railroad and to the shutdown of the plants of the American Woolen Mill Company, he exclaimed passionately:

> For months we have heard the cry, dinned and dinned and dinned into our ears, to increase production, increase production, increase production! How can increased production be accomplished under a policy of laying off thousands of workers?...The nation needs production. ...The mills and factories should run. Management should consult with the workers through the chosen representatives of the workers. The cooperation to be achieved by such a policy will give the nation the production it needs.[4]

A second and more important cause of public hostility to the labor movement was a flare-up of militancy and intransigency in the labor world in 1919, which led many good citizens to believe that the AFL had joined hands with the Soviets in a far-flung attempt to overthrow the capitalistic order. Impelled by the soaring price level, emboldened by their new sense of prestige, which government recognition had conferred, freed from wartime restraints on strikes, the unions set out militantly in 1919 to secure what they believed to be their rightful due. February brought a five-day general strike in Seattle and Tacoma in sympathy with the shipyard workers; it also ushered in a severe strike of 32,000 Lawrence textile operatives, which resulted in the formation of a rival union to the United Textile Workers — the Amalgamated Textile Workers of

[3] *American Federationist,* Oct. 1919, pp. 958–960.

[4] *Ibid.,* Oct. 1920, pp. 940–941. For similar statements see the following issues of the *Federationist:* Nov. 1919, p. 1026; Feb. 1920, pp. 157–158; Sept. 1920, pp. 846–847.

America, sponsored by the Amalgamated Clothing Workers. In August there was a strike of 65,000 employees in the Chicago stockyards and outlaw strikes in the railroad shops, which involved 250,000 men. A month later came the strikes of the Boston police and of 350,000 steel workers. In October 100,000 Atlantic longshoremen and 100,000 shipyard workers in New York left their jobs. In November 400,000 bituminous coal miners walked out for nine days, returning to work only after the issuance of a government injunction under the Lever Act. The largest strike in 1916, that of the men's clothing workers in New York, had involved only 60,000 employees; none in 1917 involved as many as 40,000; the largest in 1918 was a strike of 60,000 machinists in New Jersey; yet in 1919 there were nine disturbances each involving 60,000 or more employees and a total of 1,600,000.[5] The magnitude of the industrial upheaval of 1919 can be appreciated even better from an examination of the strike statistics[6] for the years immediately before and after:

Year	*Number of Disputes*	*Number of Employees Involved*	*Average Number of Employees per Dispute*
1916	2667	1,599,917	600
1917	2325	1,227,254	528
1918	2151	1,239,989	576
1919	2665	4,160,348	1561
1920	2226	1,463,054	657
1921	1785	1,099,247	616
1922	899	1,612,562	1794
1923	1199	756,584	631

When it is seen that the 1919 figure of 4,160,348 strikers was never surpassed nor even remotely approached in any of the adjacent years, some of the postwar "red" hysteria can more easily be fathomed. Writing in the *New Republic* for November 26, 1919, on "Is Revolution Possible," Alvin Johnson declared: "But it is the

[5]*Monthly Labor Review,* June 1920, pp. 200–201. Two of these nine not mentioned above were the Chicago building trades lockout in July involving 115,000 and the New York building trades dispute in February involving 125,000.

[6]*Handbook of Labor Statistics, 1924–1926* (Bulletin of Bureau of Labor Statistics, No. 439), p. 570. The figures include both strikes and lockouts.

strike, breaking out now here, now there, that looms largest in the fear of revolution."[7] Despite the fact that most of the disputes concerned only the usual union objectives – increased wages, shorter hours, recognition[8] – their very magnitude, coupled with the skillful work of the press in fanning the public's fear of a red revolution in America, was sufficient to taint the AFL with radicalism.[9]

Quite apart from the strikes, signs were not lacking that elements of the labor movement were actually swinging toward the left. An independent Labor Party was organized in 1919, though not with the official sanction of the AFL. That year the railroad unions took up the Plumb Plan for government ownership and democratic management of the railroads and succeeded, despite strong opposition from President Gompers and other officials, in getting the plan endorsed by the 1920 and 1921 conventions of the AFL.[10] In 1919, also, the Miners' convention came out strongly for nationalization of the mines, the Secretary pointing out that while previously "the question of the nationalization of the basic industries of our coun-

[7]*New Republic,* Nov. 26, 1919, p. 367.

[8]The principal causes of 3,253 disputes in 1919 whose causes were given by the *Monthly Labor Review* (June 1920, p. 204) were as follows:

Increase of wages	999
Increase of wages and decrease of hours	554
Recognition of union	366
	1919

[9]For the way in which the steel strike was helped to defeat by the use of "red" labels, see Commission of Inquiry, Interchurch World Movement, *Report on the Steel Strike of 1919* (New York: Harcourt Brace, 1920), Chap. 2; and *Public Opinion and the Steel Strike* (New York: Harcourt Brace, 1921), Chap. 2. Apart from propaganda of this kind, the utterances of the union officials regarding labor's demand for a share in industrial control gave color to the belief that the unions were reaching for greater power over industry. Thus the *Nation* in an article on the steel strike entitled "The Revolution – 1919" declared that the rank and file and some of the leaders had "lately ventured to challenge the entire system of control. Its members demand higher wages and shorter hours, of course; but they are thinking of the actual direction of the productive machine itself" (*Nation,* Oct. 4, 1919, p. 452). The second Industrial Conference called by the President in March 1920 reported: "There is, however, a feature of the present industrial unrest which differentiates it from that commonly existing before the war. It cannot be denied that unrest today is characterized more than ever before by purposes and desires which go beyond the mere demand for higher wages and shorter hours.... They reveal a desire on the part of workers to exert a larger and more organic influence upon the processes of industrial life" (*Report of Industrial Conference Called by the President, March 6, 1920,* p. 6 [pamphlet]).

[10]*Convention Proceedings,* 1920, pp. 283, 399–420; 1921, pp. 224, 310, 361–371.

try was more or less a visionary proposition,... today, with the action of the railway workers and through the instrumentality of the organization they have created – the Plumb Plan League – this question of nationalization comes within the bounds of those questions that can be accomplished...."[11]

In 1920, it will be recalled, the membership of American trade unions had reached a new high peak of slightly more than 5,000,000. Small wonder, then, that the public, its nerves already shaken by the revolutions abroad, viewed the rising tide of unionism with alarm.

Employers naturally seized this moment to promote the open shop as a means of deflating the gains made by organized labor during the war. Trade unionism had of course encountered open shop drives in former years. From 1903 to 1914 the AFL was constantly on the defensive against such open shop associations as the National Association of Manufacturers, the Citizens' Alliances, the Anti-Boycott Association, and various belligerent employers' organizations. Such opposition had strengthened labor's militant determination to organize.[12] While the open shop drive of the earlier period had retarded the advance of many unions, it had not thrust them back from territory already won. But the open shop movement of the postwar decade was of unprecedented severity and created a more serious problem for the labor movement.

Nowhere was the intention of employers to oppose trade unions more openly avowed than at the President's first Industrial Conference. In September 1919, President Wilson called a conference of representatives of the unions, the employers' organizations, and the public "for the purpose of reaching, if possible, some common ground of agreement and action with regard to the future conduct of industry." When the conference convened on October 6, 1919, the labor group submitted a set of principles calling for recognition of the right of wage earners to organize in trade unions, to bargain collectively through these unions, and to be represented

[11] *United Mine Workers Convention Proceedings*, 1919, Vol. 2, pp. 841–849.

[12] See, for example, *American Federationist*, Nov. 1903, pp. 1162–1164; and August 1913, pp. 600–601. The employers' associations which were actively opposed to the unions included the National Metal Trades Association, the National Founders' Association, and the National Erectors' Association.

by delegates of their own choosing.[13] The employers' group submitted a declaration in favor of the open shop, "that is, the shop in which membership or nonmembership in any association is not made a condition of employment," and emphasized the right of the employer to deal or not to deal "with men or groups of men who are not his employees or chosen by and from among them."[14]

Several attempts were made to combine the divergent points of view represented in these two statements but all failed, and the labor group withdrew from the conference. Discussing the causes for this lack of agreement, the National Industrial Conference Board, an organization endowed by employers, concluded: "In the final analysis the stand taken by the Employers' Group was predicated on the maintenance of the open shop which they regarded as a vital American principle and which they saw endangered by the type of collective bargaining insisted upon by the Labor Group."[15]

After the conference the open shop drive gathered momentum. On November 15, 1919, the *New York Herald* presented a symposium on the open shop with the views of employers in 22 leading industrial centers represented. Most of the replies were unanimous in agreeing that the open shop conferred material benefits on the employer, the employees, and the public.[16] The drive was of spontaneous origin. Special national and local open shop associations were formed, gaining the adherence of chambers of commerce, rotary clubs, bankers' and manufacturers' associations. Organizations which had never before officially professed their hostility to the unions now hung out open shop shingles.[17] In the fall of 1920 the United States Chamber of Commerce adopted by referendum vote a declaration in favor of the open shop. About the same time the National Association of Manufacturers created a

[13]National Industrial Conference, Stenographic Transcript, Fourth Day, Oct. 9, 1919, pp. 175–176.

[14]*Ibid.*, Fifth Day, Oct. 10, 1919, pp. 256–257.

[15]N.I.C.B., *Vital Issues in the Industrial Conference at Washington, D. C., Oct. 6–23, 1919* (Special Report No. 5 [1919]), p. 12. The second conference, composed of representatives of the public alone, endorsed employee representation through unions or through shop committees in unorganized establishments (*Report of Industrial Conference Called by the President, March 6, 1920*, p. 10).

[16]National Association of Manufacturers, *Open-Shop Bulletin*, No. 2, Nov. 29, 1920, p. 2.

[17]S. Zimand, *The Open-Shop Drive* (1921), *passim* (pamphlet).

special Open-Shop Department to disseminate information on the advantages of the open shop and to encourage local open shop movements.[18] A survey conducted in the fall of 1920 by the Associated Employers of Indianapolis disclosed the existence of 540 organizations in 240 cities which were actively engaged in promoting the movement. Of these 470 were styled "purely open-shop associations."[19]

The campaign gained tremendously in popular favor by advancing under the banners of patriotism and democracy. The open shop was labeled the "American Plan," thus suggesting that an establishment run on any other plan was following European and therefore, by implication, "red" precedents. To deal with organized labor was undemocratic and un-American. Some so-called "open shops" were not shops open indifferently to union and nonunion members but shops in which union membership was not tolerated. These "open shops" were thus in reality closed shops — that is, shops closed against the union. In fact some industrialists made no attempt to conceal this meaning. For example, the Secretary of the National Erectors' Association testified before the Lockwood Committee in 1920 that his organization had formally adopted the policy of the open shop which he defined as "a shop in which the foremen are expected to see to it that there are no union men."[20] And Eugene Grace, President of the Bethlehem Steel Corporation which was likewise supporting the principle of the open shop, admitted before the same committee that even if 95 percent of his employees belonged to a trade union they would not be recognized as union men.[21] The Social Action Department of the National Catholic Welfare Council summed up the matter as follows: "Not only has no 'open shop' organization declared that the 'open shop' employer would deal with the union, but every such organization that has confessed its attitude on this subject, has admitted that this practice would not be tolerated."[22]

[18] See National Association of Manufacturers, *Open-Shop Bulletin,* Nos. 1–5, Nov. 3, 1920–June 3, 1921. These *Bulletins* reprinted much testimony from employers on the greater productivity of workers in open shops, which were free from union domination.

[19] R. W. Dunn, *Americanization of Labor* (New York: International Publishers, 1927), p. 24. [20] Zimand, *op. cit.,* p. 8. [21] *Ibid.,* p. 7. [22] *Ibid.,* p. 46.

The activities of the open shop associations also revealed their antiunion bias. These included financial aid to employers engaged in contests with the unions, the use of spies and strike-breakers, the organization of shop committees, and propaganda against union tyranny and inefficiency.[23]

This widespread offensive caused President Gompers to see in the open shop movement a "plot against the unions," a "conspiracy to crush organized labor." Writing in the *New York Times* for September 17, 1922, he made his suspicions public:

> While the struggle to prevent the organization of workers has from the beginning engaged the attention of employers, there has been since the conclusion of the World War such a manifestation of united effort toward that end as to force upon any careful observer the conclusion that unusual forces have been at work and that unusual plans have been laid.
>
> The fact is, as labor sees it, that while prior to the war there was what might be termed a normal opposition to the organization of workers, there has been since the conclusion of the war an abnormal or stimulated opposition inspired and in all probability more or less actively directed from a central point.[24]

The result of this conspiracy, he pointed out, was to make it necessary for the unions "to fight for their life."

But a more serious and subtle challenge was at hand. This was the rapid development after 1922 of the art of personnel administration — a development which had gotten under way during the war, had experienced a slight slump during the depression, and had then progressed to new and higher levels of achievement. With its attempt to cultivate the good will of the working force by improving the conditions of employment, by providing some degree of security against arbitrary dismissal and the hazards of illness, old age, and death, and by creating a procedure for the airing of grievances through shop committees and other plans of employee

[23] *Ibid.*, pp. 34–35. For examples of the activities of open shop associations in various states, see *ibid.*, pp. 14–28.

[24] *New York Times*, Sept. 17, 1922. This was the leading article of the Sunday Special Features Section. Gompers listed the organizations behind the open shop drive and quoted from the speeches of the leaders. Most of his evidence was taken from Clarence Bonnett's new book, *Employers Associations in the United States* (New York: Macmillan, 1922).

representation, personnel administration aimed to furnish the workers all that the unions promised them and more. How this complicated the task of organized labor is not difficult to see. When workmen faced the militant opposition of the employers they were led to unite by the consciousness of a common foe. But the newer devices of personnel management, by binding the employee more closely to the factory, materially diminished the organizer's appeal. This is not the place to undertake a detailed history of the personnel policies of the decade, but some of the main developments can be briefly indicated.[25]

During the war, with labor scarce, wages rising, and turnover high, the industrialists began to devote serious thought to the problem of making their forces contented and efficient. In this they were aided by the government, which stimulated the study of employment management, safety, health, welfare work, and employee representation. The spurt in union power following the armistice spurred management's effort to secure labor's good will; it was desirable as a defense technique to placate the working force and avoid labor troubles in the individual plants, while at the same time the open shop drive opened a propaganda war against unionization in general.

The attempt to make industrial employment more attractive had many manifestations. The first group insurance policy had been written in 1911. In 1917 the volume of group life insurance outstanding was $346,525,000. By 1920 it had increased almost fivefold to $1,662,327,000.[26] One hundred and twenty pension plans had been adopted between 1885 and 1916; 68 more were installed between 1916 and 1920.[27] To the 60 employee stock purchase plans

[25]For excellent discussions of personnel policies the reader is referred to S. H. Slichter, "The Current Labor Policies of American Industries," *Q. J. Econ.*, May 1929, pp. 393–435; W. M. Leiserson, "Personnel Management," in *Wertheim Lectures on Industrial Relations,* (Cambridge, Mass.: Harvard University Press, 1928), pp. 125–164; and W. J. and E. K. Donald, "Trends in Personnel Administration," *Harvard Business Review,* Jan. 1929, pp. 143–155. See also the numerous studies of the National Industrial Conference Board and the Princeton Industrial Relations Section.

[26]W. Graham, "Group Insurance," *Annals Am. Acad. Pol. and Soc. Sci.,* May 1932, p. 41. The *Index* of the N. Y. Trust Co. for Nov. 1931, p. 252, gives the 1920 amount as $1,636,715,000.

[27]N.I.C.B., *Industrial Pensions in the U.S.* (1925), p. 5.

inaugurated before 1916, 111 were added by 1920.[28] There were only 12 works councils in existence prior to 1917. By 1919 their number had swelled to 225, covering 391,400 employees.[29] Another important development of this period was the transfer of authority over hiring and firing from the foreman to a centralized employment department. All these were early efforts, as the National Industrial Conference Board pointed out, to develop "a feeling on the part of employees that they are being treated right by management, that their wages are fair, . . . that any just complaint on their part will receive fair consideration by management, and that, all things considered, the plant is a desirable one in which to work."

With the defeat of the steel strikers, the textile workers, and the railway shopmen, the liquidation of war industries, and the usual demoralizing effects of a depression on union ranks, the back of labor's power was soon broken. Between 1920 and 1923 the trade unions lost 1,330,000 members – almost one half of the number gained since 1914.[30] But, while the fear of labor troubles thus largely vanished, another motive sprang up to inspire the continuance and further development of personnel administration. This incentive was the desire to cut labor costs by increased efficiency in the face of declining wholesale prices.

In 1922 nonagricultural wholesale prices stood 37 percent below those of 1920, as measured by the Bureau of Labor Statistics index. The average hourly earnings of factory workers in 24 industries, on the other hand, had declined during these years from $.61 to $.50 – a drop of only 18 percent. By 1929 nonagricultural wholesale prices had taken another tumble of 2 percent from the 1922

[28]N.I.C.B., *Employee Stock Purchase Plans* (1928), p. 2.

[29]N.I.C.B., *Growth of Works Councils in the U.S.*, Special Report No. 32 (1925), pp. 1, 5.

[30]The figures of membership are as follows:

Year	*Total Membership, American Trade Unions*	*AFL*
1914	2,716,900	2,118,500
1920	5,110,800	4,130,700
1921	4,815,000	4,041,000
1922	4,059,400	3,333,600
1923	3,780,000	3,048,600

The AFL figures are taken from the Secretary's reports to the conventions; the others are from Wolman, *op. cit.*, p. 33.

level, while hourly earnings had recovered to $.59.[31] With prices declining and wages remaining high, it became imperative to lower costs in other directions by cutting out wastes and increasing labor productivity. The recent experiences with personnel administration had demonstrated the significance of "morale" as a factor in plant efficiency.[32]

With these objectives in mind, personnel administration experienced a rapid and expanding development. In the first place, greater attention was given to the selection and handling of employees. Special industrial relations departments were organized in the larger industries. In a 1931 survey of plant industrial relations programs in 302 establishments, the National Industrial Conference Board found that 96 companies, or 31 percent of the total, had industrial relations departments or directors. Over half of the plants employing 5,000 or more employees had such departments.[33] To be sure as time went on there was a tendency to make these departments more largely advisory than administrative and to return to the foreman some of the powers which had been taken from him. But a new type of foreman was emerging, more carefully selected and trained in the art of handling men than the old "straw boss." In the investigation just cited, 28 of the 302 companies were

[31]The figures in detail are as follows:

Year	*Index Nos., Nonagricultural Wholesale Prices (1926 = 100)*	*Average Hourly Earnings of Factory Workers*
1920	154.8	$.61
1921	100.1	.53
1922	97.3	.50
1923	100.9	.54
1924	97.1	.56
1925	101.4	.56
1926	100.0	.57
1927	94.4	.58
1928	95.5	.58
1929	94.4	.59
1930	85.9	.59

Wholesale price figures are taken from *U. S. Wholesale Prices, 1930,* Bulletin of Bureau of Labor Statistics, No. 543, pp. 35–37; average hourly earnings from N.I.C.B., *Wages in the U.S., 1914–1930,* p. 44.

[32]N.I.C.B., *Industrial Relations: Administration of Policies and Programs* (1931).

[33]*Ibid.,* p. 54.

found to have formal training courses for supervisors.[34] The reduction of turnover and the prevention of indiscriminate layoff also became important features of personnel policy.[35]

In the second place employers took steps to encourage their men to save, invest, and acquire homes. According to a report issued by the Conference Board in 1929, 307 companies employing 1,322,517 workers had some type of employee thrift and investment plan. Summarizing the motives which prompted the adoption of these plans, the Conference Board remarked:

> ...it is reasonable to believe that a plan which improves the economic position of its participants increases their good feeling toward the company that sponsors it and, in some cases, contributes to it. By its character it appeals to the more industrious and substantial members of the working force and tends to influence these workers to remain with the company. This is especially true where the savings take the form of home purchase.[36]

Employee stock purchase plans also continued to be popular. Between 1921 and 1925, 162 new plans were added to the 171 inaugurated previously. In 315 companies having stock purchase plans in 1927, there were 806,068 stockholders out of 2,736,448 employees; the market value of the shares thus held was $1,045,-150,410 making an average holding of about $1300.[37] Regarding the psychology of employee stock ownership the Conference Board had this to say:

> Any number of companies have sold stock to their employees in the hope that by giving them an interest in the business they might come to feel a responsibility for their work and that a more loyal and interested labor force would be built up, that unrest would be allayed and that there would be less incentive for response to outside organizations which might seek to divide the allegiance of the workers.[38]

[34] *Ibid.*, pp. 41–45. Professor Slichter cites the Chamber of Commerce report of 933 foremanship courses in the U. S. in the year ending June 1927 (Slichter, "Current Labor Policies," p. 412).

[35] N.I.C.B., *Lay-Off and Its Prevention* (1930).

[36] N.I.C.B., *Employee Thrift and Investment Plans* (1929), pp. 74–75.

[37] N.I.C.B., *Employee Stock Purchase Plans,* pp. 2, 35.

[38] *Ibid.*, pp. 42–43. It is a serious question whether in fact employee stock ownership served these ends. The holdings were small, scattered, often without voting power and held principally by the managerial employees.

Still a third aspect of personnel policy in its relation to labor efficiency was bound up with the question of security. Since security from arbitrary dismissal and layoff has already been mentioned, we shall be concerned at this point only with group insurance and industrial pensions. The volume of group life insurance outstanding increased with enormous rapidity during the decade. In 1920 it was $1,662,327,449; in 1925, $4,299,271,187; in 1930, $9,886,028,572. In 1931 there were 38,000 master policies outstanding, covering 6,500,000 workers, with an average per capita insurance of $1540.[39] While life insurance was the most popular, some of the policies covered accidents and illness. From the employers' point of view the merit of group insurance was its tendency "to lessen labor turnover and dampen labor unrest."[40]

Pension plans also gained favor. The ultimate purpose of such plans was the improvement of industrial relations through reduction of turnover, stimulation of loyalty and efficiency, and the creation of good will and contentment. A further benefit to employers was seen in the possibility of early retirement of the superannuated. By 1925, 2,815,512 workers in 215 establishments were covered by industrial pensions.[41]

But it was a fourth aspect of personnel policy which gave organized labor most occasion for concern. This was the establishment of shop committees, works councils, company unions, and other forms of employee representation within the plant to enable the employees to gain a hearing for their grievances without recourse to an outside union agency.[42] The growth of works councils in the United States was almost entirely a product of the postwar decade. A few sporadic plans for shop representation existed before the war,

[39]Graham, *op. cit.*, p. 41.

[40]N. Y. Trust Co., *The Index*, Nov. 1931, p. 252.

[41]N.I.C.B., *Industrial Pensions in the U.S.*

[42]Technically a distinction should be made between the company union and the works council or shop committee, although the trade unions branded all forms of employee representation indiscriminately as company unions. The company union enjoyed an independent status in that the employees organization had a constitution, and an independent treasury, and enjoyed the right to elect its own officers and to negotiate written agreements covering hours, wages, and working conditions with the management. Most of the employee representation plans in the railroad shops were of this type. The shop committee, on the other hand, consisted of a handful of delegates elected periodically by the employees to discuss grievances and working conditions.

the oldest being the Filene Cooperative Association established in 1898 as an insurance committee. In 1911 the Philadelphia Rapid Transit Company devised a scheme of employee representation. The Colorado Fuel and Iron Company adopted a shop committee plan in 1915. Between 1913 and 1918, 20 firms installed the so-called Leitch Plan of Industrial Democracy.[43] But it was not until the war that the spread of employee representation plans began to assume the proportions of a movement. The necessity for uninterrupted production during the war led many manufacturers to form shop committees which could effect prompt settlement of grievances. Moreover, it will be recalled that various government agencies, such as the National War Labor Board, the Railroad Administration, and the Shipbuilding Labor Adjustment Board, had encouraged the establishment of shop committees within the plants, either with or without union recognition. In a study of 225 works councils in existence in 1919, all but 29 of which had sprung up since January 1, 1918, the National Industrial Conference Board found that 85 had been set up by the National War Labor Board, 31 by the Shipbuilding Labor Adjustment Board, and 3 by government committees, while 105 had been voluntarily adopted by individual employers.[44] These voluntary arrangements ultimately proved the more enduring.

After the war the establishment of shop committees proceeded apace, particularly in the years 1922 to 1924 when 83 company unions were formed on various railroads following the defeat of the shopmen's strike. Whereas 225 works councils were reported by the National Industrial Conference Board in August 1919, there were 725 active works councils in operation by 1922[45] and 814 in 1924.[46] The growth in the number of employees covered by such plans is shown in the following table:[47]

[43]E. Burton, *Employee Representation* (Baltimore: Williams and Wilkins, 1926), pp. 26–28.

[44]N.I.C.B., *Works Councils in the U.S.* (1919), pp. 14, 116.

[45]N.I.C.B., *Experience with Works Councils in the U.S.* (1922), p. 1.

[46]N.I.C.B., *Growth of Works Councils in the U.S.* (Special Report No. 32 [1925]), p. 5. The number of separate companies using employee representation plans, as distinguished from the number of works councils, many of which were located in the various plants of a single company, showed a decline from 240 in 1922 to 212 in 1924.

[47]*Ibid.*, p. 5. The 1926 figure is taken from an advance report of the Conference

Year	*Number of Workers*
1919	391,400
1922	690,000
1924	1,177,037
1926	1,369,078

Employee representation was most popular in public utilities, including the railroads, in textile factories, printing establishments, and metalworking plants. It was favored primarily by large establishments employing many thousands of workers where the need for representation was obviously greater than in small concerns which could afford more direct contact between the individual worker and the management. Of the 1,369,078 workers covered by representation plans in 1926, 61 percent were in companies having 50,000 or more employees.[48]

Probably the most important motive prompting the employers to establish shop committees and company unions in the early part of the decade was the desire to forestall the unions by setting up machinery through which grievances could be aired without the intervention of union officials. "There is no doubt," wrote Earl Miller in 1922, "that the non-union council movement in the United States has been largely an anti-union movement. The adoption of employee representation plans has been, in many cases, a move which has had as its immediate purpose either the undermining of existing unionism in the industry or plant, or the avoidance of unionism which appeared imminent. Moreover, these councils have generally been a success in accomplishing this purpose."[49]

Beside their usefulness as a means of adjusting grievances without union interference, another advantage was claimed for the works councils. It was held that a committee composed of workers within the establishment, and therefore familiar with the processes

Board's comprehensive investigation of employee representation (never published) given in *Law and Labor,* March 1927, p. 61.

[48]Some of the major concerns of the country, outside the railroad field, which adopted plans of employee representation were the New York Standard Oil Company, the Bethlehem Steel Corporation, the International Harvester Company, the Goodyear Tire and Rubber Company, Swift and Company, the American Telephone and Telegraph Company, and the Eastman Kodak Company.

[49]E. Miller, *Workmen's Representation in Industrial Government* (University of Illinois Studies in the Social Sciences, Vol. 10, Nos. 3, 4 [Urbana: University of Illinois, 1922]), p. 51.

of production, could be converted into an agency for promoting efficient production. On the one hand the meetings could be used to explain to the workers' delegates the financial condition of the company and to enlist their cooperation in improving its status; on the other, the delegates could be encouraged to canvass the employees for suggestions relating to improvements in industrial equipment and processes.[50] In its first report on works councils in 1919 the Conference Board found that the participation of the councils in matters affecting productive efficiency had been "relatively infrequent."[51] But three years later the Board noted a change:

> As the Works Councils became better understood, so many employers reported, there took place a gradual decrease in the use which the employees made of the works committees for the presentation of complaints and grievances and a corresponding increase in the interest which they manifested in general business conditions and plant efficiency. . . . It is evident that employers consider representation plans have a stimulating effect upon the interest taken by employees in productive efficiency.[52]

And Ernest Burton reported in 1926 that "many executives . . . who originally did not anticipate that employee representation might extend beyond a consideration of the contractual relations between employer and employee would now subscribe to the statement that it may effectively promote morale by educating both the employees and management regarding general problems of administration and management."[53]

[50]The interest of employers in securing suggestions from their workers can also be seen in the vogue which "suggestion box" systems enjoyed during the postwar decade. In 1927 over 300 concerns employing more than a million workers were using formal suggestion schemes of one kind or another. See Z. C. Dickinson, *Suggestions from Employees* (Michigan Business Studies, Vol. 1, [Ann Arbor: University of Michigan, 1927]), and his "Suggestions from Workers," *Q. J. Econ.*, August 1932, pp. 617–643.

[51]N.I.C.B., *Works Councils in the U.S.*, pp. 73–74.

[52]N.I.C.B., *Experience with Works Councils in the United States*, p. 6.

[53]Burton, *op. cit.*, p. 72. Unfortunately there is little evidence available regarding the extent to which shop committees did actually show an interest in these matters. Carroll E. French, whose study was published in 1923, found only a minority of shop committees paying any attention to problems of production. See French, *The Shop Committee in the United States* (Johns Hopkins Studies in Historical and Political Science, Ser. 41, No. 2 [Baltimore: Johns Hopkins University Press, 1923]), p. 63. Our interest in this connection, however, lies largely in the fact that shop committees were supposed to be instrumental in promoting production, thereby suggesting to the trade unions the necessity of displaying a similar interest in efficiency.

Such, then, were the principal items in the industrial relations programs of the decade, all directed, as we have already noted, to the end of reducing the costs of production not through wage cuts but by securing the good will and improving the efficiency of the working force. Out of 256 companies which responded to a request from the Conference Board for an evaluation of their personnel policies at the end of the decade, 228 expressed satisfaction, while 17 were unable to decide one way or the other. The programs, it was reported, had resulted in a better type of applicant for jobs, decreased turnover, decreased waste, fewer accidents, better health of employees, improved financial condition of the workers, increased production, and freedom from labor troubles. Most important of all was the gain in morale; 93 concerns mentioned this specifically.[54]

Obviously the personnel policies of American industry were presenting a direct challenge to the labor movement. How, in the first place, could unions appeal to workers who were already satisfied with their wages and conditions of employment? How, in the second place, could employers be persuaded to enter into collective dealings with the unions when they believed that union recognition would be inimical to the interests of productive efficiency?

There were other complicating factors. More significant, even, than the new labor policies of American industry in diminishing the worker's interest in the labor movement and in explaining the failure of the AFL to push ahead, once revival had set in, was the marked advance of real wages as the price level fell and wage rates rose. Between 1920 and 1926 real annual earnings in all manufacturing industries increased 14 percent while the membership of the AFL declined 30 percent.[55] Whereas real wages had remained

[54]N.I.C.B., *Plant Industrial Relations Programs*, pp. 90–101.

[55]The following table is instructive:

Year	*Index, Real Annual Earnings, All Manufacturing (1914 = 100)*	*Total Membership, AFL*
1920	114	4,130,700
1921	115	4,041,000
1922	120	3,333,600
1923	128	3,048,600
1924	127	2,984,700
1925	128	2,995,800
1926	130	2,879,000

almost stationary from 1895 to 1914, they advanced 30 percent between 1914 and 1926. In the early days of the labor movement when the workman had reason to feel that he was being exploited at starvation wages, that he had, indeed, "nothing to lose but his chains," the ringing cry "Toilers unite!" had infinitely more appeal than it did when the weekly pay envelope showed amazing qualities of elasticity. Foreign travelers in America during the postwar decade almost invariably commented on the worker's indifference to the union's call – a phenomenon which they attributed to the high wage policy of American industry.[56]

Finally, to complete the net of difficulty encompassing organized labor in the postwar decade, the use of the injunction in labor disputes became more frequent and more hampering, making it increasingly dangerous for the unions to employ the methods of picketing, boycotting, and even striking – techniques on which so much reliance had been placed in the early days of the movement.[57] "In the last few years," wrote President Green in 1928, "injunctions against organized labor have increased, not only in number but in extent. . . . There is scarcely any trade-union activity which has not been restrained or denied through the ever-broadening use of the writ of injunction."[58] In particular, the use of the injunction to uphold "yellow-dog" contracts created serious obstacles to organization. Whereas large concerns tended to rely upon welfare work and shop committees to stave off the union organizer, smaller firms presented their employees with yellow-dog contracts pledging them not to join a union while in the company's employ. After the Supreme Court decision in the Hitchman case in 1917, called by Green "the Dred Scott decision" of labor, such pledges

Real annual earnings are taken from P. Douglas, *Real Wages in the U.S., 1890–1926* (New York: Houghton Mifflin, 1930), pp. 239–240; membership from Secretary's reports to conventions, published in AFL *Convention Proceedings.*

Douglas points out that the increase in real wages during 1921 and 1922 was due partly to the usual lag of wages behind prices and partly to the reluctance of employers to institute sharp wage reductions for fear of provoking a revival in union strength. Moreover other ways were found to cut costs by increasing efficiency and productivity. Hence instead of high real wages being the result of increased productivity they were its cause (Douglas, *op. cit.*, p. 563).

[56]See particularly the report of the Daily Mail Trade Union Mission to the U. S. published in pamphlet form in 1927.

[57]See F. Frankfurter and N. Greene, *The Labor Injunction* (New York: Macmillan, 1930); and E. Berman, *Labor and the Sherman Act* (New York: Harper, 1930).

[58]*American Federationist*, Feb. 1928, pp. 145–146.

were entitled to legal protection from the courts and organizers could be enjoined even from persuading men under contract to join the union.[59]

From the preceding account of the capitalistic offensive in the postwar decade, it would appear that the task of organized labor grew more difficult and perplexing than ever before. Opposition to the unions took various shapes — the open shop drive, welfare programs, employee representation, yellow-dog contracts. Against this formidable array of strength, what weapons would avail? Had the time come for the Federation to revise its traditional policies in the light of a new and changing environment? That these were the questions which the leaders were asking themselves is indicated by a section from the report of the Executive Council to the 1925 convention of the AFL on "New Economic Developments":

> With the industrial changes that have come in the past few years our labor movement has found it has to meet different problems and a different type of opposition from employers who oppose the trade union movement. Made more intelligent in their methods by appreciation of industrial morale and the value of good health and safety of employees, such managements began introducing welfare work and so-called employee representation plans. . . .
>
> These methods therefore constitute new problems which our movement must study to establish the facts and findings, and the results of our studies will help us to find the best way of meeting the problems and the dangers they entail. Thus we shall develop the tactics and methods with which to cope with our new problems. It is useless to continue to use tactics and methods adapted to organization of industry and methods of opposition based upon conditions that existed in previous decades. The unions that make progress against existing difficulties must be able to match brains against brains and information and resourcefulness against information and resourcefulness.[60]

The new tactics and methods which evolved from this realistic approach will be the subject of succeeding chapters. Here it may

[59]See J. Seidman, "The Yellow Dog Contract," *Q. J. Econ.*, Feb. 1932, pp. 348–361; C. Cochrane, "Why Organized Labor Is Fighting 'Yellow Dog' Contracts," *American Labor Legislation Review*, Sept. 1925, pp. 227–232; "The 'Yellow Dog' Device as a Bar to the Union Organizer," *Harvard Law Review*, April 1928, pp. 770–775; and *Convention Proceedings*, 1925–1931.

[60]*Convention Proceedings*, 1925, p. 33.

be briefly noted that the policy which the AFL and some of its constituent unions found it most expedient to adopt was that of respectability. Instead of trying to storm the portals of industry by using the old strike technique, the labor movement decided to attempt a quiet and respectable admission by emphasizing the constructive functions of the union — their interest in scientific management, waste elimination, and industrial efficiency — all matters dear to the hearts of industrialists in the postwar years and likewise of no small interest to the public. Where militancy could not force an entrance, the more subtle strategy of cooperation might persuade employers to open the gates voluntarily to the unions. "The trade union movement," said President Green before the Harvard Union in 1925, "has been passing through that period when physical controversies and the tactics of force were most effective; it is now in a period when its leaders must seek the conference room, and there, by exposition and demonstration, convince conferees of the justice and wisdom of Labor's position."[61]

But before presenting the record of the official pronouncements of the AFL on the subject of cooperation and productive efficiency, it is necessary to trace the change in the relation between scientific management and organized labor after the war. In view of the marked hostility which characterized their prewar relationship, their postwar reconciliation forms an interesting and significant chapter in the history of trade union interest in production.

[61]Green, *Modern Trade Unionism* (1925), pp. 13–14 (pamphlet).

CHAPTER V

The Reconciliation between Organized Labor and Scientific Management

I see. . . before the labor movement a great future as I also see a great future before the engineering profession. If the engineer should join hands with the workman,. . .each day will have increasing opportunities to develop those human functions which are essentially intelligent. . . .If you study the laws of humanity with the same degree of intensity that you study the laws of material science, you will render a tremendous service, and, as President of the American Federation of Labor, it is my firm conviction that the labor movement not only welcomes but invites your cooperation."[1]

THUS Samuel Gompers indicated the abandonment of the prewar attitude of organized labor toward scientific management and the engineering profession. Only four years earlier he had denounced the engineers in no uncertain terms; now he held out his hands and invited their cooperation. Signs of an impending reconciliation had been present during the war when service on government boards threw engineers and labor leaders together, enabling each to get a better grasp of the other's point of view. But several years more were required to develop a real sense of accord.

[1]From an address by Gompers, "Industry and the Engineer," delivered before the American Society of Mechanical Engineers," Nov. 5, 1920, reprinted in *American Federationist,* Dec. 1920, pp. 1109–1111.

The first evidence of a change in union attitude was a resolution passed by the 1919 convention of the AFL favoring scientific research and the technical application of the results of research to industry. Calling the increased productivity stemming from scientific research "a most potent factor in the ever-increasing struggle of the workers to raise their standards of living," and pointing out that there was a limit beyond which standards of living could be advanced not by "the usual methods of readjustment" but only by "the utilization of the results of research in industry," the resolution called upon the government to foster a broad program of scientific and technical experimentation.[2]

In December 1919, the Executive Council of the AFL, acting in conjunction with the officials of the Railway Brotherhoods, invited representatives of the trade unions and farmers' organizations to a conference in Washington to consider the problems facing the labor movement and to recommend appropriate solutions. The results of the conference were embodied in a document entitled *Labor, Its Grievances, Protests and Demands,* reaffirming the right to strike, protesting against the autocratic policy of the Steel Corporation, denouncing the use of the injunction in labor disputes, and pleading for democracy in industry.

> Labor is fully conscious [read the manifesto in part] that the world needs things for use and that standards of life can improve only as production for use and consumption increases.... There can not be a full release of productive energy under an autocratic control of industry. There must be a spirit of cooperation and mutuality between employers and workers. We submit that production can be enhanced through the cooperation of management with the trade union agencies which make for order, discipline and productivity....
>
> To promote further the production of an adequate supply of the world's needs for use and higher standards of life we urge that there be established cooperation between the scientists of industry and the representatives of organized workers.[3]

This suggestion of an alliance between engineers and trade unionists led the American Academy of Political and Social Science

[2]*Convention Proceedings*, 1919, pp. 319–320. For endorsements of this resolution see *American Federationist,* Jan. 1920, pp. 68–70.

[3]*American Federationist,* Jan. 1920, pp. 37–38. See also *Convention Proceedings,* 1920, pp. 67–68.

to sponsor in 1920 a volume of papers representing the points of view of the "scientists of industry" and the "organized workers." The symposium, issued under the title, "Labor, Management and Production," was jointly edited by Morris L. Cooke, Samuel Gompers, and Fred J. Miller, President of the American Society of Mechanical Engineers – in itself a collaboration of no small significance. Commenting on the importance of the volume, Cooke declared: "In the following pages almost for the first time the recognized spokesmen of organized labor in this country take an unequivocal stand for production as being in the interest of the wage earner. There is no other single development possible in industry which by comparison could be as important.... Such a volume as this would have been altogether impossible before the war."[4]

There was general agreement among the contributors that the most pressing problem of the moment was an increase in industrial production, both to repair the wastages of the war and to bring down the cost of living. It was also agreed that one solution to the problem lay in earnest cooperation between the technicians and the workers. Several years earlier the engineers would have asserted that production was peculiarly a function of management, that labor could make no significant contributions to industrial technique, and that the worker's prime job was obedience to commands from his superiors. Now the hold of this autocratic concept of industrial relations began to relax. In "Labor, Management and Production" the engineers stressed the importance of affording the workers a chance to use their "creative" powers in industry. "Every Worker an Engineer" – the title of one contribution – typified the new point of view. There was, moreover, ample recognition of the desirability of giving labor a voice in industrial management, of securing labor's consent to changes in managerial policy – statements which reflected in the first place the failure of the old driver method of industrial management during the war when jobs were many and men were few, and in the second place the insistent demand of a powerful labor movement for more democracy in industry.[5]

[4]"Labor, Management and Production," *Annals Am. Acad. Pol. and Soc. Sci.*, 91 (1920), viii–ix.

[5]*Ibid.*, articles by H. W. Shelton and F. J. Miller in particular.

Several years earlier the union leaders for their part had been indifferent to the exigencies of production and hostile to the activities of the engineers. Now Gompers, Woll, and Frey – all old war horses of the Federation – were proclaiming that "the workers of America are fully conscious that the world needs things for use and that standards of life improve only as consumption increases."[6] They declared their conviction that "to the idealism and aggressiveness of the labor movement the technical skill and the inventive genius of the engineer are fitting and needed complements."[7] But, while thus affirming their readiness to cooperate with the technicians in increasing output, they demanded in return that production be carried on for use and not for profits alone, that the workers be assured a decent livelihood and humane treatment, and that the unions participate jointly with the engineers in determining working methods and standards of production.[8]

The desirability of cooperation between the unions and the engineers was ably elaborated by the "intellectuals" contributing to the symposium. On the one hand, they advised the unions that the exercise of power entailed responsibility and that higher wages could best be secured by increasing output; on the other, they pointed out to the engineers that the unions could make significant contributions to industrial efficiency. Unions could set up safeguards in the form of wage and employment guarantees necessary to assure the individual worker's interest in production; union negotiators possessed expert knowledge of production problems; finally, the unions could exert disciplinary powers over members who persisted in slowing down on the job.[9] While little attention was paid by any of the contributors to ways and means of making cooperation effective, it is significant that the volume reflected a change in the attitude of engineers and trade unionists toward each other. The more practical work of implementing the desire for cooperation with specific machinery could well be left for a later date.

[6] *Ibid.*, p. 8.

[7] *Ibid.*, p. xi.

[8] *Ibid.*, pp. 57–58; 140–145.

[9] *Ibid.*, pp. 79–88; 40–49. The "intellectuals" here cited were Professor Leiserson and H. B. Drury, then a member of the Industrial Relations Division of the U. S. Shipping Board and formerly a member of the Economics Department of Ohio State University.

Further evidence of labor's shifting point of view with respect to production and scientific management was the publication in the *American Federationist* of March 1920, of a feature article by H. B. Drury, "Labor and Production," which Morris L. Cooke had commended to Gompers' attention. There were three roads, wrote Drury, along which organized labor might advance:

1. The more abundant production of material goods.
2. Distribution of goods already produced.
3. Improvement of working conditions and the status of labor in industry.

All of these roads, he declared, were important; but, whereas in the past the second had been the most traveled, organized labor would gain more in the future by frequenting the first and third, since by 1920 labor had gained or was in a position to gain "not far from as large an income as the state of production will permit." As labor organization was extended, he continued, there would be less room for fighting and more for constructive endeavor. But what specifically could labor do to increase production? "The most fundamental thing that organized labor as such could do," he said in answer to this question, "would be to advance as its own the general philosophy that production is the goal of industry. . . ." The main task of the labor movement in this regard was the education of the rank and file in the importance of productive efficiency. Secondary measures included the elimination of strikes as far as possible and union promotion of technical changes in industry both through acquiescence in the introduction of new devices and methods and through original suggestions for technological improvements.[10] By making production their goal, he pointed out, the unions would enrich the workers, enhance their interest in their jobs, and materially improve the status of organized labor in the community. When it is recalled how scornfully Gompers some years earlier had rejected Professor Laughlin's advice that the unions take an interest in production, the significance of the publication of Drury's article can more easily be appreciated.

In November 1920 came Gompers' speech before the American Society of Mechanical Engineers, "Industry and the Engineer."

[10] *American Federationist,* Feb. 1920, pp. 237–244.

That month, speaking in similar vein before the Preliminary Conference on Industrial Research, he stated: "Labor is not opposed to increased production or to improved methods. Quite the contrary. We recognize there can be no permanent betterment of standards of living for all except by increasing the things that contribute to better and more satisfactory living."[11]

Toward the end of 1920, when the open shop drive was getting strongly under way, the Executive Council of the AFL called in Herbert Hoover and Robert Wolf "to secure the new engineering point of view and to hold counsel with engineering spokesmen concerning the outlook for the immediate future" – an outlook which was then distinctly unpromising. "It will be a mistake," said Gompers in reference to this consultation,

> for anyone to suppose that engineers are possessed of a magic power. ...Not all of them are even so much as in sympathy with the movement of the workers. But great numbers of them...are ardently desirous of pooling their thought and effort with the thought and effort of whosoever may be seeking...to in some degree moderate the injustices in industry and develop democratic thought in industry. To such the men and women of Labor will always go for interchange of thought and for the joining of hands insofar as may be possible for the good of all.[12]

The next important landmark in the history of the relations between scientific management and organized labor was the publication in 1921 of *Waste in Industry*. This volume was the outcome of a proposal made by Herbert Hoover to the council of the Federated American Engineering Societies in February 1921 that a representative group of engineers make a survey of industrial wastes and recommend practical steps for their elimination. In assaying the relative responsibility of labor and management for uneconomical production the committee found that over 50 percent of the responsibility could be laid at the door of management and less than 25 percent at the door of labor.[13] Among its recommendations the committee suggested that labor organizations do their share in eliminating waste by "studying the needs of the industries in which

[11] *Ibid.*, Dec. 1920, p. 1112.
[12] *Ibid.*, Jan. 1921, pp. 34–35.
[13] Federated Engineering Societies, *Waste in Industry* (New York: McGraw-Hill, 1921), pp. 8–9.

they earn a livelihood and allying themselves with the technicians who serve with them to increase production – which will inure to the ultimate benefit of all."[14]

This report commended itself favorably to Gompers and other Federation leaders, probably because of its light assessment of labor's responsibility for industrial waste. At the Unemployment Conference called by Secretary Hoover in 1921 Gompers introduced three resolutions, one proposing that "all parties accept the challenge implied in the report on the Elimination of Waste in Industry by the Federated American Engineering Societies and join in the practical work of eliminating causes of high production costs in industry." At the 1922 convention of the AFL the Executive Council referred to *Waste in Industry* as "the first constructive effort in the world. . . to disclose the nature of industrial wastes," and stated that the unions were eager to eliminate waste in order to reduce unemployment.[15] And at the 1925 convention the committee on wages urged cooperation between labor and management in eliminating such wastes of production as were disclosed by the Engineering Societies' report so that selling prices might be lower and wages higher.[16] But an essential condition of such cooperation, it was pointed out, was the unquestioned recognition of the wage earners' right to organize.[17]

After Gompers' death Mr. Green continued his predecessor's attitude of friendliness toward the engineering profession. On December 3, 1925, he addressed a joint meeting of the Taylor Society and the Management Division of the American Society of Mechanical Engineers on "Labor's Ideals Concerning Management."

In touching upon Labor's ideals concerning management [he stated] we are conscious of the fact that we have been and are now passing through a period when changes are taking place. These changes affect human relationships in a most vital way. Many of our older concepts are giving way to the newer and more progressive points of view.... Labor is understanding more and more that high wages and tolerable

[14]*Ibid.*, pp. 27–28.
[15]*Convention Proceedings,* 1922, pp. 75–76.
[16]*Ibid.*, 1925, p. 231.
[17]See, for example, Frey's speech, "Eliminate Industrial Waste," in *American Federationist,* Oct. 1921, pp. 835–843.

conditions of employment can be brought about through excellency in service, the promotion of efficiency and elimination of waste.[18]

The occasion was equally noteworthy in revealing the more liberal attitude of the adherents of scientific management toward the unions. It would be hard to imagine either Frederick Taylor or the early members of the Taylor Society, with their bitter hostility to organized labor, welcoming a president of the AFL to their midst, still harder to imagine Taylor endorsing the eulogy published by the Taylor Society after Gompers' death in which the labor chieftain was referred to as an "industrial statesman" whose "ideal was human welfare – construction, not destruction."[19]

But perhaps the most dramatic manifestation of the changed relations between scientific management and organized labor was afforded by the Trade Union Conference on Elimination of Waste in Industry held in Philadelphia, April 9–10, 1927. Sponsored jointly by the Philadelphia Labor College and the Philadelphia Central Labor Union, this was the first conference ever organized by a group of trade unionists to which engineers and employers were invited to discuss the problem of waste elimination. Among the engineers present were M. L. Cooke, F. J. Miller, and Geoffrey Brown, while the union representatives included William Green, Matthew Woll, and delegates from some of the textile and printing organizations. In opening the conference, Israel Mufson, Secretary of the Philadelphia Labor College, declared:

Labor is not satisfied with demands for wages only but is concerned about some control in industry; to help reorganize it more efficiently; to make possible the use of its intelligence towards better practices within industry in order to gain greater benefits for itself and those dependent on it. And in order to learn how these ends may be accomplished the conference we are now opening has been planned.[20]

While most of the papers dealt rather generally with such topics as labor's interest in waste elimination, workers' participation in job study, and the relation between scientific management and organized labor, several described in detail some specific instances of

[18]*Bulletin Taylor Society,* Dec. 1925, pp. 242–246.
[19]*Ibid.,* Dec. 1924, p. 240.
[20]*American Federationist,* June 1927, p. 667. Practically all of this issue is devoted to the conference. The papers were also reprinted in pamphlet form by the AFL.

union cooperation in waste elimination. Commenting on the significance of the conference, the Executive Council reported to the 1927 convention of the AFL: "Such forums are to be commended as opportunities to let wider circles know the achievements possible through cooperation of unions and management as well as for the stimulus to our movement itself."[21]

More important, however, than speeches and forums was the actual working alliance between engineers and trade unionists in developing concrete plans of union-management cooperation. In at least two instances trade unions participated in job analysis and the establishment of standards of production through time-study technique.[22] The most famous cooperative experiment — the B. and O. Plan — was fathered and nurtured by an engineer, Otto Beyer. Another engineer, Geoffrey Brown, was employed by the AFL in its Southern organizing campaign in 1930.

Turning from these evidences of the change in labor's attitude toward scientific management, we have now to inquire into the influences responsible for the new point of view. Why was it that Gompers' hostility to engineers, so pronounced in 1916, gave way a few years later to friendliness and consultation?

One of the causes, already indicated, was the wartime cooperation between engineers and trade unionists on government councils. In particular the friendship which sprang up at this time between President Gompers and Morris L. Cooke was of signal importance in calling Gompers' attention to certain problems of production and efficiency which he had hitherto largely ignored, and in making him see that not all engineers were bloodless scoundrels interested in nothing better than cracking whips above the heads of cowering workmen.[23] It was Cooke who secured Gompers' collaboration in editing "Labor, Management and Production," who persuaded Gompers to publish Drury's article "Labor and Production," who arranged for Gompers' appearance before the American Society of Mechanical Engineers. In June 1920, an article by

[21] *Convention Proceedings,* 1927, p. 37.

[22] I refer to the Cleveland and Naumkeag experiments, in both of which Mr. Cooke was largely concerned.

[23] Interviews with Mr. Cooke and with Miss Florence Thorne, who corroborated Mr. Cooke's statements concerning his friendship with and influence on Mr. Gompers.

Cooke entitled "Will Labor Make the Next Move?" appeared in the *New Republic.* Pointing out that real democracy in industry involved not only a voice in managerial decisions but also a share in responsibility for economical production, Cooke advised the labor movement to hire its own production engineers to confer with experts retained by the management over acceptable procedures for increasing plant efficiency.[24]

But this and similar exhortations might have exerted little influence had it not been for certain fundamental reforms in the theory and practice of scientific management itself which were instrumental in removing some of the basic grounds of labor's opposition.[25] Two of the principal union criticisms of scientific management, it may be recalled, were (1) that scientific management was largely mechanistic in its attitude toward workmen, robbing them of all creative interest in their work and treating them not as human beings but as so many cogs in a machine; and (2) that scientific management allowed the workers through their unions no voice in the determination of either production standards or basic wage rates.

Fortunately, as we have seen, the postwar literature of scientific management laid increasing stress upon industrial psychology, upon the "human element in production," the "creative instinct in industry," and the relation between efficiency and consent.[26] The streams which fed this psychological current were both the wartime exposure of the deficiencies of the old driver method of management and the efforts of a few of the more progressive members of the Taylor Society to call to the attention of the engineering profession the shortcomings of any system of management which neglected the intelligent faculties of the workman and relied exclusively on pecuniary incentives to secure maximum efficiency. The pioneer efforts of Robert Valentine and Robert Wolf in this re-

[24]*New Republic,* June 9, 1920. See also Cooke's *An All-American Basis for Industry,* a pamphlet reprinting some articles appearing in the *Philadelphia Public Ledger,* April 14–17, 1919; and his article "Organized Labor and Research," in the *American Federationist,* August 1927, also reprinted in pamphlet form.

[25]For an excellent account of these changes see George Filipetti, *Industrial Management in Transition* (Chicago: Irwin, 1946).

[26]See the chapters dealing with labor in *Scientific Management in American Industry,* ed. H. S. Person (New York: Harper, 1929).

gard have already been touched upon. After the war the work was carried on primarily by Wolf, M. L. Cooke, O. Beyer, and Geoffrey Brown – all of whom made numerous inroads into the citadels of orthodox scientific management by constantly urging before the Taylor Society the importance of enlisting the workman's interest in job analysis and appealing to his creative abilities for suggested improvements in industrial processes.[27] Other engineers also began to reflect the new point of view. Thus Henry L. Gantt, once a proponent of the more dictatorial form of scientific management, confessed in his *Organizing for Work,* published in 1919, that "the 'efficiency' methods which have been so much in vogue for the past twenty years in this country, have failed to produce what was expected of them. The reason seems to be that we ignored the human factor and failed to take advantage of the ability of the ordinary man to learn and to improve his position."[28] And Harlow Person, who in 1917 had been rather doubtful of the value of consulting workers in regard to managerial policies,[29] declared in 1920:

> The successful, that is the productive management of the future must conceive of the workers... "not as the working man but as the man working"; as an individual with technical knowledge to be utilized, instincts for self-expression to be given expression, intellect to be given the opportunity for development, interest in the purposes, policies and methods of production to be regarded.[30]

It was this new emphasis of scientific management on the necessity of treating the worker as a human being which helped to allay Gompers' earlier distrust of the engineers. "Evidences are not lacking," he said to the American Society of Mechanical Engineers in 1920, "that engineers are seriously seeking to realize the ideals they

[27]See for instance Mr. Brown's paper, "Workers' Participation in Management," read before the Dec. 1928 meeting of the Taylor Society and published in *Bulletin Taylor Society,* Feb. 1929, as well as his numerous contributions to the *American Federationist.* In the *Bulletin Taylor Society* for June 1925 (pp. 142–144) there is an interesting account by Robert Wolf of his use of charts rather than bonuses as incentives in the paper industry. While Mr. Cooke was still a firm believer in time study and production standards, Mr. Beyer believed that the interests of efficiency were best furthered not through the use of a stop watch, but through getting the men to make suggestions for improvements in working methods.

[28]Gantt, *Organizing for Work* (New York: Harcourt, Brace and Howe, 1919), pp. 89–90.

[29]*Bulletin Taylor Society,* Feb. 1917, p. 4–5.

[30]"Labor, Management and Production," p. 139.

have formulated. During the past year your representatives of engineering organizations as well as individual engineers have come to me, seeking help in getting a better understanding of the human element essential to production."[31] In January 1921 Gompers again expressed appreciation of the engineers who were "giving broad recognition...to the human side of the equation."[32] And a few months later he wrote: "The labor movement is hopeful...today because there are abundant signs that the engineers and scientists have recovered from and progressed far beyond that pseudo-science that brought them such ill-repute among workers a decade ago when 'speed up' was their watch word and when humanity was classed with steel and wool as material for the production of goods."[33]

Beside the new emphasis of scientific management on the human element in production there was a weightier reason for its growing acceptability in labor circles. This was the more cordial attitude which the engineering profession was beginning to display toward organized labor after the war. Valentine, in the earlier period, had emphasized the desirability of enlisting the cooperation of the unions, but his had been "a voice crying in the wilderness."[34] Not until labor had acquired a more powerful status as the result of its wartime activities did the engineers give signs of recognizing the labor movement as an important factor in industrial relations which might be capable of constructive activities. This recognition was not confined to invitations to labor chieftains to address engineering conventions nor to speeches expressing a general willingness to afford labor a voice in industrial management, although their significance must not be too lightly assayed. More important were the concrete experiments being evolved by such engineers as Cooke, Brown, and Beyer to afford the unions a chance to participate in time study and the determination of production standards, as well as the development of a technique of union-management cooperation to elicit suggestions from workers for ways and

[31] *American Federationist*, Dec. 1920, p. 1109.
[32] *Ibid.*, Jan. 1921, p. 34.
[33] *Ibid.*, June 1921, p. 470.
[34] It is interesting to note that Valentine advised the members of the Taylor Society to read Webb's *Industrial Democracy*, Marot's *American Trade Unionism*, and Cole's *The World of Labour*. See *Bulletin Taylor Society*, Jan. 1916, p. 12.

means of improving quantity and quality production.[35]

The gradual shift in point of view which such practices represented was vividly brought home by Cooke's address before the Taylor Society in December 1928, on the occasion of his retirement from the presidency. Eleven years before Cooke had severely criticized union opposition to time-study and bonus systems and had denied that scientific management could be predicated on a basis of group consent.[36] Instead of adapting scientific management to the needs of the labor movement he had urged the unions to conform to the requirements of scientific management. Now, after practical experience with joint research had shown him the wisdom of modifying some of the earlier, more autocratic tenets of the Taylor system, he chose as the subject of his address "Some Observations on Workers' Organizations." Announcing that he had come to look upon "a virile labor union movement as a social necessity," he suggested that engineers had a responsibility not only for recognizing but also for encouraging the organization of workers.

> If [he remarked] we should come to look upon some organization of the workers, such as labor unions, as a deep social need, might it not develop that practices, however otherwise enlightened they may be, which withdraw any group of employes from the support of such organizations may become anti-social? If such proves to be the case, any employer setting up working standards even above those demanded by labor organizations and resisting the effective organization of his employes, may in fact be acting without a due regard for this deep social need.

[35]See especially Cooke's paper on the Cleveland experiment: "Morale as a Factor in Time Study Technique," in *Bulletin Taylor Society,* April 1927. On Feb. 5, 1926, the Taylor Society devoted an entire meeting to the topic of union-management cooperation in the railway industry, Otto Beyer, Bert Jewell, and Sir Henry Thornton being the speakers. The Naumkeag experiment was described at the Dec. 1929 meeting. See *Bulletin Taylor Society,* April 1930, pp. 63–79.

[36]Cooke, "Who is Boss in Your Shop?" *Annals Am. Acad. Pol. and Soc. Sci.,* May 1917, pp. 167–185. The central idea of this paper was that the group should follow the leadership of an informed individual. In industry run by labor unions, Cooke pointed out, this would be impossible if the unions were "so organized that everything has to be decided by group action" (p. 177). And further he remarked: "But to advocate in industry a type of labor unionism which prohibits the use of the stop watch and the payment of rewards for high performance is to advocate ultimate industrial slavery — however novel the type" (p. 181).

More concretely he proposed that the engineers assist in developing a place and function for workers' organizations in industry, the elements of such a functional status to include inspection, suggestion, review of time study, and participation in job analysis.[37]

How far the disciples had traveled beyond the master can also be seen from the subsequent efforts of the Taylor Society to frame an industrial code conforming to the best managerial practices in the United States.[38] The revised version of the code, which came up for discussion at the spring meeting of the Society in 1931, declared that time-and-motion studies should be " a joint enterprise between labor and management," that employment should be made more secure through the gradual introduction of technological changes, guarantee funds, and the dismissal wage, and that satisfactory relations in industry could be developed only through "definite group organizations of the workers" necessary to create a condition of confidence among the employees. Expanding this last point, the code continued:

Labor's right to recognition as a party to collective agreements is now, in this country, so widely recognized as to be generally beyond debate in theory and beyond contest in practice. That right may be exercised through various forms of organizations which can, however, perform the function of representing the employes only if control of the workers' organization rests fully and really with the workers themselves.[39]

The fact that the Society still hesitated to give its unqualified support to independent rather than so-called "company" unions would indicate that the great majority of members had not yet been converted to an enthusiastic endorsement of organized labor. On the other hand, it must not be inferred that the unions themselves bestowed unqualified approval upon all practices of scientific

[37] *Bulletin Taylor Society,* Feb. 1929, pp. 2–10. Although describing himself as "holding rather pessimistic views as to the significance of the company union movement," Cooke apparently hesitated, in view of the prejudices of the Society, so to word his remarks as to exclude the company union from consideration. "I want primarily," he remarked, "to evaluate the group idea and only incidentally to discuss the way in which company unions, or standard unions or any other form of group organization may give the idea vitality" (p. 3).

[38] In June 1930 the *Bulletin Taylor Society* announced the appointment by President Kendall of an Industrial Code Committee, headed by Mr. Cooke and including engineers, industrial relations directors, educators, and editors. A tentative draft of the code was discussed at the Dec. 1930 meeting. See *Bulletin,* Feb. 1931, pp. 19–30.

[39] *Ibid.,* Oct. 1931, p. 185.

management. Most labor organizations still opposed the use of the stop watch, while others refused to countenance the introduction of bonuses or other forms of incentive-wage payment.[40] But both sides undoubtedly had approached each other more closely than an impartial observer present at the hearings on scientific management in 1914 would ever have supposed possible.

Beside the more cordial attitude of scientific management toward organized labor, there was another factor helping to explain the readiness with which Gompers, Green, and other union officials sought the company of engineers. Efficiency of production, as was pointed out in the last chapter, became the shibboleth of American industry during the postwar decade. The labor movement, meanwhile, was suffering from the charge of restriction of output; it was facing the competition of company unions and the new personnel policies of progressive establishments. Strategic considerations therefore seemed to indicate to labor the desirability of displaying a like interest in efficiency, waste elimination, and job analysis, and of hiring its own technical experts to offer engineering services to management. In brief, labor's changed point of view with regard to scientific management was dictated by the exigencies of its situation. It was an adaptation made to meet a new environment and new problems; as such it represented merely an extension of the opportunistic philosophy which had characterized the AFL since the early days when Gompers, Strasser, and other leaders set to work to fashion a labor movement in harmony with the requirements of American life.

[40]Mr. John Frey, Secretary of the Metal-Trades Department of the AFL, who was the labor representative on the Hoxie committee investigating scientific management in 1915, later stated his belief that time study with union participation is an acceptable procedure in rate and task setting, providing no claim is made for strict accuracy and that proper allowances are made for individual variations in efficiency. He was, however, firmly opposed to bonus systems (interview, Jan. 27, 1932).

→ CHAPTER VI ←

The AFL and Union-Management Cooperation: Official Statements

UNION-MANAGEMENT cooperation became one of the important planks in the AFL platform after the war. Expressed in the simplest and most general terms, union-management cooperation means the participation of labor organizations in the task of finding better and more economical methods of production.[1] Like labor's changed attitude toward scientific management, described in the preceding chapter, union-management cooperation was a part of the Federation's new policy of respectability — the effort to

[1]Strictly speaking, of course, union-management cooperation means some such arrangement as obtained under the B. and O. Plan, where shop committees jointly representing the unions and the management discuss suggested improvements in industrial processes and shop working conditions. The term was added to the Federation's vocabulary in 1925 when the B. and O. Plan was first receiving prominence. But, while the AFL spokesmen usually meant by union-management cooperation an arrangment similar to the B. and O. Plan, they gradually gave the term a wider meaning to embrace other instances in which unions showed a concern for productive efficiency. Thus the Executive Council in its report to the 1928 convention pointed out that the forms which such cooperation might take varied greatly: "...sometimes it is a joint educational project to provide skilled workers for the trade or industry, sometimes an employment service that connects these workers with employers,...sometimes a contribution to administrative problems, or participation in improving production standards, the regular adjustment of misunderstandings and difficulties that come in all live situations, and finally systematic cooperation with management to make production effective" (*Convention Proceedings*, 1928, p. 42).

emphasize the constructive potentialities of the labor movement as a means of making the unions more palatable to employers. Once collective bargaining over wages and standards of employment had been established, the trade union, it was declared, would naturally turn its energies into constructive channels and concern itself with problems of production. Only an independent union, the argument continued, could supply the broad basis of confidence essential to honest cooperation. Hence trade unions were superior to company unions. Such, in brief, was the argument developed by the AFL to meet the new labor policies of American industry.

The present chapter deals with the pronouncements of the AFL on union-management cooperation and the closely allied topics of industrial democracy and company unionism, and with the Federation's new wage policy and its relation to trade union interest in production. The use of union-management cooperation in the Southern organizing campaign will be treated in a subsequent chapter.

The Idea of Union-Management Cooperation as Set Forth in Federation Literature

Broadly speaking, the idea of union-management cooperation as set forth in Federation literature developed through two distinct phases. In the first phase, which sought to counter the open shop drive of 1920–1923, the technical term "union-management cooperation" had not yet been born. The idea, nevertheless, was present. It was during this period, as has already been pointed out, that Gompers and other members of the Executive Council began to emphasize the interest of trade unionism in productive efficiency and to draw elaborate pictures of a new order of industrial democracy in which labor and management would cooperate to produce goods for service rather than for profits alone. Behind this proffer of cooperation there was evident a desire to dispel the hostility manifested in accusations of restriction of output, in the open shop drive, and in compulsory arbitration laws. Moreover, the strike upheavals of 1919 and 1922 had made a policy of conservatism and respectability expedient in order to offset the charge of radicalism loosely brought against the whole labor movement. Much, if not all, of the talk of cooperation at this time was vague and amorphous, expressing a general ambition rather than reflecting any concrete achievement. No attempt was made by the Federation to evolve a definite scheme for making cooperation effective or to indicate specific machinery for utilizing the much vaunted constructive potentialities of the trade unions. But this, of course, was to be expected. A technique of cooperation could be hammered out only in the practical workaday world of the shops, not in the council rooms of the AFL.

The second phase began about 1924 when the promising evolution of the B. and O. Plan furnished both a name and a technique for cooperation. Henceforth the Federation could speak more concretely and with greater assurance concerning the constructive functions of organized labor. As other experiments got under way, the Federation turned from uttering pious hopes to publicizing substantial developments in union-management cooperation. In the meantime, although the open shop drive had subsided, the more subtle challenge of company unionism had appeared. Hence, in this period union-management cooperation was widely advertised by the AFL as the answer to company unionism.

The World War, as was noted in an earlier chapter, threw an intense emotional aura about the word "democracy" and left the labor movement, in the full confidence of its newly acquired prestige, demanding immediate recognition of the principle of democracy in industry. The Reconstruction Program of the AFL called for a participation of the workers in determining the laws affecting them in industry equivalent to their participation as citizens in determining legislative enactments.[2] It is questionable, however, whether anything more was meant by this fine flow of rhetoric than that workers should insist upon their right to organize and to bargain collectively through their trade unions. It was merely a case of pouring old wine into new bottles in the hope that a more attractive label might create a wider market.

But as the shortage of commodities began to be reflected in the high cost of living, for which a large part of the blame was cast upon the restrictive practices of the trade unions, and as employers

[2] *Ibid.*, 1919, p. 71.

banded together to deflate the gains which labor had made during the war, the demand for industrial democracy took on a new significance. The full cooperation of all factors of production for the attainment of maximum output, it was pointed out by AFL spokesmen, required a substitution of democracy for autocracy in industry. Autocratic control, typified by the open shop drive, was powerless to release productive energy. Production could be enhanced only by industrial democracy, by cooperation between management, the unions, and the technicians. Industrial democracy, moreover, meant production for use, not for profit alone. "The ideal of America," read the manifesto, "Labor, Its Grievances, Protests and Demands," "should be the organization of industry for service and not for profit alone. The stigma of disgrace should attach to every person who profits unduly at the expense of his fellow men."[3] The labor movement, continued this document, was anxious to increase production provided the increase was used for service rather than for enrichment of the owners of industry. The AFL was thus putting itself forward as the would-be savior of industry, as the friend rather than the enemy of production. This was clearly revealed by a section of the report of Executive Council to the 1920 convention, headed "Constructive Demands."

"Such emphasis has been laid by employers upon the need for increased production," the report began, "that we believe a presentation of the trade-union point of view in relation to production should be placed before the nation in authoritative manner." There followed a denial of the accusation that labor was restricting output, the diminution in stocks being attributable to the devastation of the war and to the autocratic policies of employers. Organized labor, the report went on, desired a voice in the management of industry; it wanted shop committees, a chance for self expression in work, an opportunity to be consulted about the reconstruction of industry. To the attainment of these ends, the Executive Council recommended

> the setting up of conference boards of organized workers and employers thoroughly voluntary in character and in thorough accord with our trade union organizations as means of promoting the democratization

[3] *Ibid.*, 1920, p. 67.

of industry through the development of cooperative effort. We point out to employers the fact that industry which is the life blood of our civilization can not be made the plaything and pawn of a few who by chance today hold control. Industry is the thing by which all must live and it must be given the opportunity to function at its best.[4]

In 1921, as the pressure of the employers' offensive became more and more severe, the Federation leaders grew alarmed. "The workers," cautioned Gompers, "have need to be alert and militant, for never in the history of the American labor movement has plutocratic greed presented such an organized menace to democratic progress."[5] But the Federation had a rather new conception of "militancy." For when the Executive Council summoned a conference to discuss a labor situation which was "more serious and more menacing...than...any that has existed in the history of the trade union movement," the conference answered the challenge of the employers by emphasizing the cooperative functions of the union. "The labor movement," reported the meeting, "offers those voluntary and conciliatory methods of negotiation, arbitration and agreement through which it is possible to develop in our industrial life the highest degree of good will and the highest degree of productivity."[6]

As the open shop drive continued, Gompers constantly reiterated the interest which organized labor had in production — an interest which would find expression, once industrial democracy had been assured. Thus in 1922 he asserted:

Labor's utmost thought always is the improvement of the processes of production, the perfection of service, the elevation of the standards of life for all. If we can presently emerge finally from the contests against autocratic domination of industry into which we were plunged by the deliberate planning of powerful combinations of high finance and great industries after the war, we shall enter upon a period of development and progress such as we have never known. The arts of the producer are the arts that thrill our soul.[7]

By 1923 Gompers had evolved a concept of industrial democracy

[4] *Ibid.*, 1920, pp. 86–88.
[5] *American Federationist*, Jan. 1921, pp. 52–53.
[6] *Ibid.*, April 1921, pp. 295–297.
[7] *Ibid.*, Oct. 1922, p. 739. See also issues of June 1921, p. 477; Feb. 1923, p. 151.

that extended far beyond the boundaries of collective bargaining. The new ideal, which closely approached syndicalism, was concretely formulated in a section of the report of the Executive Council to the 1923 convention of the AFL, entitled "Industry's Manifest Duty."[8] "We feel that the hour has struck," the document began, "for a pronouncement of the aims of labor that shall more nearly express the full implications of trade unionism than has yet been undertaken in these annual reports." The close of the war, it was pointed out, marked a turning point in human relations – it gave to the labor movement a larger function in society.

> Henceforth the organization of the workers into trade unions must mean the conscious organization of one of the most vital functional elements for enlightened participation in a democracy of industry whose purpose must be extension of freedom, the enfranchisement of the producer as such, the rescue of industry from chaos, profiteering and purely individual whim, . . . and the rescue of industry also from the domination of incompetent political bodies.

To avert government intervention, industry must save itself. But only through the divorce of management from financial control and through the formation of a cooperative alliance between organized workers, organized managers, and organized technicians could a rescue be effected:

> It is not the mission of industrial groups to clash and struggle against each other. Such struggles are the signs and signals of dawning comprehension, the birth pangs of an industrial order attempting through painful experience to find itself and to discover its proper functioning. The true role of industrial groups, however, is to come together, to legislate in peace, to find the way forward in collaboration, to give of their best for the satisfaction of human needs. There must come to industry the orderly functioning that we have been able to develop in our political life. . . .

No one group, however, should exert dominant control. Industry, so organized, must fix upon production and service as its goals, not upon profits which represent the interest of a single factor.[9] But in

[8] *Convention Proceedings*, 1923, pp. 31–34. See also the *New York Times*, July 23, 1922 for an article by Gompers, "The Fundamental Issues."

[9] Labor's policies for the attainment of industrial democracy, it was stated by the Committee on Resolutions at the 1924 convention, "can be understood only in connection with labor's utter inevitable and irreconcilable opposition to the conduct of

demanding a thorough reorganization of industry along democratic lines labor was not unmindful of its responsibilities and obligations: "It is more than collective bargaining that is required. In sending up its voice for a great constructive democratization of industry Labor is not asking for a chance to get. Labor is asking for a chance to *give*. There will be enough for *all* when it comes to getting."[10]

Similarly, in suggesting the principles that should govern the organization of the power industry along the lines laid down in "Industry's Manifest Duty," Gompers proposed "that trade unions shall develop full responsibility for negotiating all agreements determining wages, hours and conditions of work, for educating employes in the methods and processes of cooperation for the elimination of industrial waste and the development of more efficient production and for assuring a square deal to the workers."[11] Just how the union as a union could make a greater contribution to industrial efficiency than could be secured from unorganized workers was never specifically indicated by Gompers, aside from the rather general assertion that "the trade union is a repository of the industrial experiences of its members."[12] But the planning of details and the diagraming of procedures were not, he pointed out elsewhere, the proper function of the AFL. The Federation could merely set forth a philosophy; only time and experience could "develop the actual detailed methods and bring into being the condition for which the policy calls."[13]

Meanwhile time and experience were already at work building up a specific technique of union-management cooperation through an elaborate system of joint committees in railroad shops. By the summer of 1924 Gompers was able to point to the success of the B. and O. Plan as constituting "a knockout blow to the arguments of those who say that it is impossible for employers and organized

industry exclusively or fundamentally for profit. Industrial democracy must be as clearly defined by what it moves away from as by what it moves towards" (*Convention Proceedings,* 1924, p. 256).

[10] *American Federationist,* May 1924, p. 401.

[11] *Ibid.,* August 1924, pp. 627–628.

[12] *Ibid.,* p. 625.

[13] *Ibid.,* May 1924, p. 399.

labor to work in closest cooperation."[14] The report of the Executive Council to the 1925 convention contained for the first time a section entitled "Union-Management Cooperation." The B. and O. Plan, it was pointed out, demonstrated the truth of labor's assertion that, once the right of collective bargaining had been recognized, the unions could turn their attention to constructive activities. The Council suggested that the movement be given serious study and consideration and recommended that the Federation keep in touch with engineers and industrial experts who might be helpful in developing the information and procedures necessary to the establishment of union-management cooperation.[15]

An even longer section of the Council's report was devoted to this subject the following year and was concerned principally with proving that unions were essential to any genuine participation of the workers in solving problems of production. The unions, it was declared, established standards which made for confidence, stability, and good will; they assumed responsibility for group discipline; they were interested in maintaining standards of craftsmanship and output – in all these ways they could make significant contributions to industrial efficiency. In thus asserting its readiness to cooperate, organized labor was not seeking to appropriate the functions of management, but merely to supplement them:

> Management secures the finances, makes ready the plant, keeps abreast technical progress, purchases, plans and directs. To use the materials which management supplies, man the machines, and carry out plans, workers are employed. They bring to the factories creative ability and labor power necessary to supplement the preparations of management. . . . This is obviously a relationship that calls for cooperation, a cooperation that is to all intents and purposes a real partnership in a work undertaking.

More specifically the Council recommended the establishment of joint shop committees charged with responsibility for working out problems of production, such committees to be different from the agencies concerned with the settlement of grievances.[16]

[14] *Ibid.*, July 1924, pp. 574–575. See also issues of June 1924, p. 484; Oct. 1924, p. 813; Jan. 1925, p. 32.

[15] *Convention Proceedings*, 1925, pp. 35–36. This was part of a larger section headed "New Economic Developments."

[16] *Ibid.*, 1926, pp. 51–52.

In its report for 1927 the Council specified in detail those activities of labor organizations which might be labeled "constructive." These included:

Agencies for interpreting collective agreements
Arbitration based on research
Joint determination of production standards
Joint undertakings for educating craftsmen
Union supervision of production
Presentation of unsatisfactory working conditions
Joint committees to consider improvements in operating efficiency.[17]

It appears from the first two items in this classification that the Council did not conceive of union-management cooperation as a function strictly separate from that of collective bargaining in the usual sense of the term – the making, interpreting, and enforcing of a joint agreement. But in general the Federation leaders spoke of cooperation as a further stage in the development of collective bargaining, one which was not to be confused with the settlement of grievances. Put very briefly, the "theory" of the labor movement which the AFL was expounding was as follows: The primary function of a young and unrecognized union is the establishment of collective bargaining through militant insistence on the right of the workers to a certain standard of wages, hours, and working conditions. Once this fighting stage has been successfully passed, however, the union assumes a new and responsible function in industry. Militancy gives way to cooperation, insistence on rights to acknowledgment of obligations; machinery for the settlement of grievances is supplemented by machinery for the consideration of ways and means of making production more effective.[18]

As the ideas of the Federation were gradually clarified and given substance by the development of specific projects in union-management cooperation, of which the B. and O. Plan afforded the most dramatic example, [19] their public affirmation was stimulated by the challenge of company unionism.

[17] *Ibid.,* 1927, p. 36; cf. 1928, p. 42.

[18] See, for example, Green's speech, *Modern Trade Unionism,* reprinted by the AFL.

[19] A detailed description of the B. and O. Plan by Sir Henry Thornton, Otto Beyer, and President Wharton of the machinists' union was the outstanding feature of the 1929 AFL Convention, while the Naumkeag experiment was outlined before the 1930 meeting.

It appeared to the Federation that the publicizing of specific experiments in union-management cooperation would be immensely serviceable in persuading employers to recognize the cash value of dealing with organized labor. Business unionism was once more surging to the fore. The ardent fervor for industrial democracy had burnt itself out by 1925. Passions excited by the war had had time to grow cool. Moreover, the death of Gompers in 1924 removed the leader who was chiefly responsible for labor's brief plunge into Utopia construction. Thereafter the Federation no longer concerned itself with the reconstruction of industry on the basis of production for use rather than profits alone. Instead it became anxious to demonstrate that "the union is a good business proposition for wage earners and employers jointly."[20] This desire to prove the dollars-and-cents superiority of the trade union represented a gradual and grudging admission on the part of the AFL that company unions had been promoted not alone to thwart the labor movement but also to improve plant morale and efficiency.

As was pointed out previously, the 1918 convention of the AFL had endorsed shop committees in the belief that they would be controlled by the unions. When it become apparent a year later that works councils were being heralded as antidotes to trade unions, the Federation took alarm and adopted a resolution introduced by the steel strike organizers vigorously condemning all plans of employee representation as undemocratic and ineffective and advising its members to have nothing to do with them. "It is evident," stated the resolution in part, "that company unions are unqualified to represent the interests of the workers, and that they are a delusion and a snare set up by the companies for the express purpose of deluding the workers into the belief that they have some protection and thus have no need for trade union organization."[21] And in 1920 the Executive Council bitterly assailed the President's Second Industrial Conference for attempting "to give encouragement and permanency to the various forms of company unions and shop organizations and various forms of so-called employee representation, whose chief merit is that they serve the purposes of the

[20] *Convention Proceedings,* 1930, p. 82.
[21] *Ibid.,* 1919, pp. 302–303.

employers by organizing the workers away from each other."[22]

By 1925, however, the Federation had begun to realize that mere denunciation of the company union would not make it vanish magically from the industrial world. It was growing aware of the claim that employee representation plans had a beneficial effect upon output and was thus coming to see that the trade union, if it wished to survive, must demonstrate its superiority over the company union in the matter of promoting efficiency. The first important indication of this point of view was the recommendation of the Executive Council to the 1925 convention of the AFL that a study be made of the actual operation of company unions, "so we may plan the best way of dealing with them."[23] Such a factual investigation was imperative because "employers are spreading the fiction that company unions are necessary to provide channels for cooperation between management and employes in production problems."[24]

Another indication was President Green's leading editorial in the *Federationist* for October 1925, "Company Unions Not Enough," which read in part:

> Certain employers claim that the company-union makes possible cooperation between management and workers in production problems. Such cooperation with unions they claim is impossible, because as they say, unions are organized for militant purposes only. There is no justification for this declaration, for employers themselves made it necessary for unions to employ defensive and militant purposes and methods. ...There are convincing proofs of the economic value of union-management cooperation, which demonstrate that the cooperation between company unions and management is most superficial.[25]

At the 1926 convention the challenge of the company union was declared to be one of the most serious problems facing the labor movement. Union-management cooperation was labeled the "answer" to company unions. "Your committee believes," reported the Committee on Resolutions, "that the time is ripe for the American labor movement to work progressively for the substitu-

[22] *Ibid.*, 1920, p. 85.
[23] *Ibid.*, 1925, p. 34.
[24] *Ibid.*, p. 230.
[25] *American Federationist*, Oct. 1925, pp. 873–874.

tion of union-management cooperation for company unions.... To accomplish this will require continued effort over a period of time and our method of approach must be based upon careful and scientific study of the situation supported by an aggressive, concentrated and well-directed campaign."[26] More particularly, it was suggested that the President of the Federation arrange for a study of the comparative results of union-management cooperation and company-union cooperation. After the achievements of these two policies had been analyzed and classified, the Federation would then "be in a position to let facts speak for themselves."[27] The convention endorsed these recommendations and authorized the Executive Council to levy a specific assessment on national unions to provide funds for the study.[28]

That the problem was one to be solved by a fact-finding and educational campaign rather than by conflict was the opinion reiterated at subsequent conventions. For example, the Executive Council reported in 1928:

> We believe that the effective way to refute the claims of proponents of so-called employee representation plans is to show why these plans are based on a wrong understanding of human nature and human relations and to submit evidence of the constructive results of union-management cooperation.
>
> Good business men can not permanently resist cooperative relations with an agency that offers results in elimination of industrial wastes, higher quality standards of production, improvements in operating machinery, and constructive suggestions based on experience and reflection.[29]

Although nothing that could strictly be called a "scientific" investigation of the comparative merits of company unions and union-management cooperation emerged from Federation headquarters, through speeches, conferences, pamphlets, and articles the AFL gave wide publicity to various experiments in cooperation undertaken by its members. The Trade Union Conference on the Elimination of Waste in Industry has already been mentioned.

[26]*Convention Proceedings*, 1926, p. 287.
[27]*Ibid.*, p. 318.
[28]*Ibid.*, p. 291.
[29]*Ibid.*, 1928, p. 115; cf. 1927, pp. 42–43.

Another example of this type of strategy was afforded by the publication of the union brief in the I.R.T. injunction suit of 1928.[30] Prepared by Professor Oliphant of the Columbia Law School and bolstered by some 50 affidavits submitted by labor experts, this document dwelt at length upon the superior advantages of the trade union, citing as proof numerous illustrations of union-management cooperation which, to use the words of the brief, had "gone beyond the usual trade agreements covering wages, hours, working conditions and adjustment of grievances, to constructive cooperation to increase production, eliminate waste and maintain continuity of service." The company union was termed at best a "promising experiment," but one needing to be supplemented by collective bargaining with an independent trade union which alone could establish the feeling of security and confidence necessary to release creative interest and energy on the part of the workman.[31]

But it was in the Southern organizing campaign of 1930 that the idea of *selling* trade unionism to management by the offer of constructive cooperation found its most dramatic application. This, however, is a subject which must be deferred to the following chapter. Meanwhile another facet of the idea demands attention. While it was as an organizing device that union-management cooperation commended itself most highly to the AFL, a further gain to labor was seen in the possibility of securing higher wages from increased efficiency of production. This brings us to a consideration of the "new wage policy" of the AFL.

The "New Wage Policy" of the AFL

No analysis of the idea of union-management cooperation would be complete unless some reference were made to the "new wage policy" of the AFL. Lest it be thought, however, that it was an

[30]This was an action brought by the Interborough Rapid Transit Company of New York City against the Amalgamated Association of Street and Electric Railway Employees of America and William Green, *et al.*, for an injunction to restrain the defendants from attempting to organize the plaintiff's employees, who not only already belonged to a company union, the Brotherhood of I.R.T. Co. Employees, but who, in 1927, had signed yellow-dog contracts pledging themselves not to join any outside organization for two years. The injunction was not granted.

[31]H. Oliphant, *Interborough Rapid Transit Company against William Green, et al.: Brief for Defendants* (New York: Workers Education Bureau, 1928), *passim.*

intellectual conversion to the productivity theory of wages which caused labor to turn its attention to problems of production – a conversion for which Laughlin and other economists, it will be recalled, had labored hard and intently before the war[32] – it should be remarked at the outset that the "theories" of the AFL were more apt to reflect than to determine its policies and methods of procedure. Since the days when Gompers and Strasser were hammering out a labor movement to "fit" American conditions, the Federation had never been guided in the formulation of policies by abstractions evolved in the scholar's study. Its intellectual concoctions had a more pragmatic flavoring. Theories were adopted to explain policies which had been shown in practice, or were assumed, to have desirable consequences for the movement as a whole. In the early years of the labor movement, for example, the strategic utility of a bargaining theory of wages in building up the armies of labor directed the Federation's wage philosophy toward the channels of distribution. In the postwar decade the possibilities of union-management cooperation in advancing the cause of labor called for a serviceable theory relating wages and production, in order to enlist the interest of the rank and file in the new policy of cooperation by the promise of higher wages, and to justify future demands for wage increases on the basis of labor's constructive contributions to efficiency.[33]

Although the new wage policy was not officially enunciated until the Atlantic City convention of 1925, the doctrine had been foreshadowed in the years just preceding. In 1920, for example, Mr. Frey had written: "The American trade-union movement is fully aware of the fact that wages depend upon production,"[34] and that same year President Gompers had declared in words strangely echoing those of Professor Laughlin and President Eliot: "But however erroneous may be some of the opinions on the subject,

[32]See Chap. 1, *supra*.

[33]While the new wage policy was a helpful corollary to the policy of union-management cooperation, it should be pointed out that probably the most important stimulus to the evolution of the theory was the continued decline of the price level during the decade which robbed the old cost-of-living wage argument of all its efficacy.

[34]"Labor, Management and Production," *Annals Am. Acad. Pol. and Soc. Sci.*, 91 (1920), 144–145.

wages are paid out of production and out of nothing else."[35]

At the Denver convention in 1921 the Executive Council stressed the need for a new wage policy. The principle that wages should be adjusted solely with reference to the cost of living – a principle which had been serviceable to the movement when prices were mounting skywards, but which was now proving equally serviceable to employers during the depression – was flatly rejected. Although it was unprepared at that time to describe the particular mold in which a new wage theory might be cast since careful research alone could reveal an appropriate principle, the Executive Council did give some indication of the kind of theory for which it was groping:

> Ultimately, we feel, there must be found some method of relating standards of living to social usefulness or production service, though under present industrial management this has not yet been found possible on any just basis....
>
> There are but two avenues leading to permanent higher standards of living for our people as a whole. One of these is the elimination of waste, either in the form of mismanagement or of undue exploitation and profiteering. The other is increased productivity. Both must be traveled simultaneously.[36]

In accepting this report the convention authorized the appointment of a committee to undertake the formulation of a "comprehensive, well-considered theory capable of real service in the practical problem of determining wages."[37]

The following year the Executive Council reported that the task of finding a wage theory was being hampered both by lack of funds and by lack of scholars to study the actual process of wage determination. The committee had finally resorted to the expedient of requesting college professors who were teaching courses in labor problems to send their students to union headquarters to work over wage data.[38]

It was thus not until 1925 that a definite pronouncement on

[35] *American Federationist,* April 1920, pp. 357–358.

[36] *Convention Proceedings,* 1921, pp. 68–69.

[37] *Ibid.,* 1922, p. 34. The committee appointed by Mr. Gompers included James Duncan, chairman, M. F. Ryan, William Green, A. J. Berres, John Frey, Matthew Woll, and Samuel Gompers.

[38] *Ibid.,* pp. 34–35.

wage theory was forthcoming. In the convention of that year the Committee on Resolutions, expanding a statement by the Executive Council, declared, first, that the interests of the wage earners and of the whole populace as well were promoted by increasing the quantity and improving the quality of production and by high wage standards necessary to maintain the purchasing power of the workers. In the second place, the Committee advised unions to oppose all wage reductions, urging upon management "the elimination of wastes in production in order that selling prices may be lower and wages higher. To this end we recommend cooperation in study of waste in production. . . ." Although a mild version of a productivity theory of wages might have been inferred from this statement, Delegate Frey rose to express his dissatisfaction with the report, declaring that it left the whole question of wage theory still vaguely defined. He therefore moved the following amendment to the Committee's statement: "Social inequality, industrial instability and injustice must increase unless the workers' real wage, the purchasing power of their wages, is advanced in proportion to man's increasing power of production." Strenuous objection to this amendment was immediately raised by Matthew Woll, who said that it sought "to adopt a theory or school of wages known as the productivity school of wages" and that he for one was unwilling to have the Federation adopt a declaration which would commit it irrevocably to one school of thought. "Indeed, I am led to believe," he continued, voicing a time-honored opinion, "that the less we have to do with theory in these matters, the better off we are, because we find ourselves confronted with all sorts of conditions, circumstances and environment, and we find oftentimes that theory will lead us nowhere, while our crude judgment expressed in trade union activities has gained more for us." Delegate Lynch of the Typographical Union then suggested that increased production should lead to shorter hours as well as to higher wages. After a lengthy debate the matter was referred back to the committee. As finally adopted by the convention the resolution included both the Frey and the Lynch amendments.[39]

Probably no other action of the Federation up to that time had

[39] *Ibid.*, 1925, pp. 36, 231–233, 271.

evoked such a round of applause from outsiders as this wage declaration brought forth. Economists, engineers, editors, business men – all saw in the resolution the final triumph of their efforts to steer the philosophy of organized labor into sound economic waters. Yet it is doubtful whether the full significance of the declaration was appreciated by the Federation at the time of its adoption. Only calm and casual reference, for instance, was made to it in an editorial in the *American Federationist* for November 1925, which pointed out that the various portions of the report "were not submitted as an inclusive or definite theory of wages but as standards or indexes to serve in lifting wage negotiations to more definite and better informed bases."[40] Gradually, however, the thunder of applause awoke the Federation leaders to a better appreciation of the position they had taken. Frey, for example, congratulated the convention in 1927 "upon being the first trade union movement to open the book of sound and true economics,"[41] while President Green, before the same convention, rhapsodically hailed the wage declaration as "the beginning of a new era – a position far in advance of any we have ever taken before."[42]

To what extent was it true that the declaration represented a new departure in union philosophy? Neither the idea that production was the source of wage increases nor that unions should cooperate in eliminating waste could fairly be termed startling by an attentive observer who had followed the speeches and writings of the Federation spokesmen since 1920. The basic element of novelty inhered in the final portion of the declaration – the proposition that real wages should advance "in proportion to man's increasing power of production." According to an explanatory pamphlet issued by the Federation in 1927, this rather ambiguous statement was interpreted to mean that, whereas in earlier periods labor had striven first for higher *money* wages and later for higher *real* wages, it must henceforth strive for higher *social* wages, "for wages which increase as measured by prices and productivity."[43] "For, higher

[40]*American Federationist*, Nov., 1925, p. 1006.

[41]*Convention Proceedings*, 1927, p. 198.

[42]*Ibid.*, p. 217.

[43]AFL, *Organized Labor's Modern Wage Policy*, Research Series No. 1 (1927), p. 9 (pamphlet).

productivity without corresponding increase of real wages means that the additional product has to be bought by others than the wage earner. This means that the social position of the wage earner in relation to other consumers becomes worse, because his standard of living will not advance proportionately with those of other groups."[44]

In other words, organized labor must be concerned with seeing that, at the very least, labor's share in the national dividend did not become smaller. To assist in the application of this theory to the practical problems of wage determination, the *Federationist* began in 1927 to publish monthly indexes of labor's share in production and consumption, together with studies of particular industries, showing the extent to which labor's share in the value added by manufacture had varied over a period of years. Individual unions that found their share in productivity decreasing because of "unjustifiable" increases in the shares of other factors were advised to press for an increase in wages.

But it is the relation of the new wage policy to union-management cooperation that especially concerns us here. What the 1925 wage declaration may be said to have accomplished in this connection was the provision of a respectable and convincing rationale indicating the motives which might lead unions to interest themselves in production. For, with increased productivity formally recognized as an important source of wage advances, it followed that labor had a powerful incentive to aid management in improving efficiency and eliminating waste. As the Executive Council pointed out in its 1926 report, trade unions were concerned to maintain and increase standards of production, because "increased production is recognized as a basis for wage increases."[45] The importance of this reasoning must not be overlooked. It was particularly essential for the leaders in winning the consent of the rank and file to the policy of cooperation to demonstrate how such a policy would redound to labor's own benefit. Obviously trade unionists could not be led to support a plan which promised merely to augment the profits of capital.

[44]*Ibid.*, p. 17.
[45]*Convention Proceedings*, 1926, p. 51.

Looked at from another angle, union-management cooperation provided an argument with which labor could establish its claims to a share in the gains of increased efficiency. To be sure, there was nothing in the wage declaration suggesting that labor was entitled only to those gain which it had created. This was no marginal productivity explanation of wages in the conventional sense of the term. As Frey said with reference to the new wage policy, "It is not merely a question of what labor may be entitled to. It is largely a question of the volume of wages which must be paid unless industry and commerce desires to strangle itself. . . ."[46] Nevertheless, it stood to reason that, if labor could point to substantial contributions in the way of improving efficiency, its plea for wage increases was likely to find a more sympathetic ear before impartial tribunals. In many of the wage briefs prepared by the Labor Bureau, Inc., for unions which engaged in various projects of union-management cooperation – the Cleveland Garment Workers' Joint Board; System Federation No. 30, Baltimore and Ohio Shopmen; and the Salem Sheeting Workers' Local No. 33 – the fact of such cooperation was adduced as a major argument in behalf of the equity of higher wages.

From this survey of the declarations of the AFL on wages and production, it appears that the philosophy of the labor movement had undergone a new orientation since the days when the cry of the toilers was for "more, more, more." The cry of the toilers was still for more, but there was added the sobering corollary that to get more labor had to help in producing more – a principle which Gompers had once sarcastically scored as the abstract musing of a professor shut up within library walls. Whether the new theories would afford as powerful a force in strengthening the ranks of organized labor as the older philosophy which acknowledged no obligations but merely asserted a militant determination to make increasing demands upon industry remained to be seen. It may be said, however, in answer to those who at the time were skeptical of the rallying strength inherent in the new policies, that they were addressed not to the nonunion workman but to the nonunion em-

[46]*American Federationist,* March 1931, p. 290. See also *Convention Proceedings,* 1927, p. 197. This interpretation was confirmed in an interview with Mr. Frey.

ployer. The new technique of organizing advocated by the AFL consisted of "selling" the union to the employer rather than to the worker. Instead of storming the portals of industry by rousing the workers to band themselves against their employers, the Federation now emphasized the cash value of trade unionism in the hope that employers might thereby be led to open the gates voluntarily to the unions. Whether this policy was likely to accomplish any significant results in the way of organization can best be judged from a consideration of the use of union-management cooperation in the Southern organizing campaign.

→ CHAPTER VII ←

Union-Management Cooperation and the Southern Organizing Campaign

ON JANUARY 6, 1930, a conference of several hundred union delegates in Charlotte, North Carolina, launched the great crusade to organize the South. The decision to spread the tenets of unionism into the industrial regions below the Mason and Dixon line had been made by the Toronto convention of the AFL in the fall of 1929. It followed a spontaneous revolt of thousands of textile operatives in Tennessee and the Carolinas during the spring and summer against certain grievances of long standing – a 60-hour week, a weekly pay envelope of $9 or $10, unsanitary working and living conditions – and, more immediately, against the introduction of the "stretch-out" system.[1] According to Dr. Broadus Mitchell the stretch-out system was "the match which set off the powder

[1]Under the "stretch-out" system the number of looms or spindles assigned to each operative was increased with little or no increase in pay. Although extra assistance was usually given the spinner or weaver, the system involved a reduction in the total working force and hence a decrease in unit labor costs. Before the disturbances of 1929, Southern textile manufacturers had increased the number of looms per weaver from 24 to 48 and in some cases to 76. Subsequent testimony of these manufacturers revealed that the system had been inaugurated in a thoughtless manner without any prior consultation with the operatives. See U. S. Senate Committee on Manufactures, *Working Conditions of the Textile Industry in North Carolina, South Carolina and Tennessee: Hearings* (1929), particularly the testimony of President Smith of the Brandle Corporation.

train of strikes in the cotton-mill South,"[2] while an organizer of the United Textile Workers declared that its introduction did more to hasten the progress of unionization than twenty years of organizing effort.[3]

Yet little of permanence in the way of organization had resulted from these uprisings. In South Carolina the strikes were conducted by local leaders with outside union assistance neither desired nor forthcoming. In Gastonia, North Carolina, the Communistic National Textile Workers took command of the situation, while in Elizabethton, Tennessee, and Marion, North Carolina, the operatives summoned organizers from the United Textile Workers and the AFL to their aid. Regardless of the type of leadership, the strikes all failed to achieve any extension of collective bargaining. In every case the armed force of the militia, aided by injunctions, evictions, mob murders, and kidnappings, was able to crush the sparks of rebellion. These drastic measures were then supplemented by minor concessions in working and living conditions designed to immunize the employees more completely against "Northern radicals and agitators." At the first signs of union activity Southern industry and government had struck back with vigor and assurance.[4]

In view of the weakness of the UTW, its failure to plant a permanent organization in the South at this time was not surpris-

[2]B. Mitchell, "The Present Situation in the Southern Textile Industry," *Harvard Business Review,* April 1930, p. 302.

[3]*American Federationist,* Jan. 1930, p. 25. From 1903 to 1918 the United Textile Workers had sent organizers to the South, had chartered a few short-lived locals each year, and had fought some bitter strikes at Atlanta in 1914, Anderson, in 1916, and Columbus, Georgia, in 1918 — all without securing any foothold in Southern mills. But in 1919 and 1920 the country-wide labor unrest, the government's policy of union recognition, the prosperity of the cotton industry, and the strength of the United Textile Workers in the North led to a sudden spurt in Southern organization. During the first eight months of 1919 the UTW chartered 67 new locals in the South and by October of that year it claimed 40,000 paid-up members in North Carolina and 5000 in South Carolina. But the depression of 1921, with its train of unsuccessful strikes against wage cuts, pricked the balloon of organization so sharply that by 1927 George S. Mitchell doubted whether the UTW had as many as 2000 paid-up members in the South. See Mitchell, *Textile Unionism and the South* (Chapel Hill: University of North Carolina Press, 1931); and H. M. Cassidy, *Trade Unionism in the South* (Editorial Research Reports [July 20, 1929]).

[4]For a dramatic account of these strikes see Tom Tippett, *When Southern Labor Stirs* (New York: Cape and Smith, 1931). See also D. McCracken, *Strike Injunctions in the New South* (Chapel Hill: University of North Carolina Press, 1931).

ing.[5] If the labor movement was to take advantage of the seething spirit of unrest among southern workers, it was clear by the fall of 1929 that the UTW could not work unaided. It needed the financial and moral support of the whole labor movement. This the 1929 convention of the AFL, after listening to a report by the Executive Council on the "Awakening South" which suggested that all unions include the South in their organizing campaigns and after devoting a full morning session to speeches by striking textile operatives and organizers fresh from the field, decided to bestow.[6] The convention authorized the Executive Council to raise funds to organize the South and directed it to call a conference of officials of the 102 national and international unions to lay plans for the campaign.

In accordance with this mandate a preliminary meeting was held in Washington on November 14, 1929. It recommended that all national unions assign at least one organizer to the South, their efforts to be coordinated under the direction of the President of the AFL, and that the Federation appeal for contributions to aid the United Textile Workers.[7] The first formal conference to inaugurate the campaign was held in Charlotte on January 6, 1930, with President Green as the presiding officer and with 229 members present, including organizers from 26 national unions, local workers from 96 different crafts, and representatives of city centrals, state federations of labor, and the AFL. Although the Southern spokesmen stressed the exploitation of the workers and sharply urged the necessity for a militant campaign, the general temper of the meeting was conservative, reflecting the Federation's new policy of respectability. Only ten years before another large-scale campaign had been directed by the AFL, that one to organize the steelworkers. At the time of the earlier offensive the labor movement had bristled with talk of workers' control and the reorgan-

[5]Although the UTW had boasted a membership of 104,900 in 1920, by 1922 this number had dwindled to 30,000 – a figure which remained constant for the rest of the decade. About one half of this membership was employed in the hosiery industry; most of the remainder were in highly skilled novelty and specialty lines – tapestry, carpets, etc.; only 1% or 2% were employed in the basic cotton and woolen industries, chiefly in Salem and New Bedford.

[6]*Convention Proceedings,* 1929, pp. 59–60; 265–283.

[7]*Ibid.,* 1930, pp. 83–85.

ization of industry, with repeated warnings that hard fought strikes would follow should labor's demands be ignored. No such militant notes were sounded at the Southern conference. The *New York Times'* headline summary of the meeting, "Green, Voicing Friendship for Employers, Asks Their Aid at Charlotte Session—No Strikes to Be Called," was eloquent of the change which a decade had wrought in the temper and strategy of the labor movement.[8] For almost two hours Green spoke on "Labor's Message to the South." Flaying the Communists as a destructive "force that would destroy our country, that would strike at the very soul of our institutions," he sketched the contrastingly peaceful mission of the AFL, as one which sought merely to convince the South of the advantages of collective bargaining and to acquaint it with the constructive contributions which the unions were ready and able to make to industrial efficiency and prosperity:

> We believe [he announced] that if, in this great Southland, we are permitted to function, we can make a distinct contribution toward the development of efficiency, of cooperation and of understanding between employers and employes here. We are here for that purpose. We come with the hand of friendship extended to you. There is no sword in our scabbard. There is no weapon in our hand. We come not with the mailed fist but with the open hand to the employers of the South appealing to them to give us the opportunity, to try us out and see whether we can help this industrial situation in the South.[9]

It was to be an organizing and educational campaign, with no strikes or unreasonable demands to arouse the apprehensions of the public and the industrialists.

What factors dictated the adoption of so rational and conservative a policy? In the first place, the general language of cooperation had been in the mouths of the Federation leaders for almost a decade. The Southern campaign now afforded an excellent opportunity to apply the formula of union-management cooperation to a specific situation in the hope that it might prove an "open-sesame," swinging wide the gates of Southern industry to organized labor. In the second place the UTW was not able and the AFL not authorized to finance a series of strikes in the South. With its

[8] *New York Times,* Jan. 7, 1930.

[9] Green, *Labor's Message to the South,* p. 16 (pamphlet reprint).

shrinking membership and treasury and its failure to penetrate the textile mills of the North after the strike disasters of 1921 and 1922, the UTW was plainly in no condition to furnish strike relief. While the Federation had been authorized to make a general appeal for organizing funds, this was very different from a systematic plan of assessment to build up a war chest. But if militancy was apt to involve the labor movement in expensive commitments, the policy of cooperation labored under no such disadvantage. Finally, the enormous obstacles in the way of organizing the Southern textile industry made a new procedure well worth trying. These difficulties concerned both the workers and the mill owners. Aside from periodic outbursts of rebellion like those of 1929, Southern operatives had been largely apathetic towards labor organizations. The presence of immense labor reserves back on the farms among the hills, the contemporary unprofitableness of farming which made industrial work even at miserably meager wages seem attractive,[10] the background of strong mountaineer individualism, the system of mill-village paternalism and employee welfare work – all contributed to the indifference, not to say suspicion, with which union organizers were regarded in cotton-mill regions.[11] There were other complicating factors, the negro problem, the preponderance of woman and child labor, the lack of a stable factory population. But more serious than any of these was the bitter and uncompromising hostility of employers, of the press, and of the public to organized labor – a hostility born of the desire to attract Northern capital by advertisement of a "cheap and contented" labor source unpolluted by union affiliations.[12] Add to this the widespread belief that all trade unions were branches of the Third

[10]The average yearly earnings of a farm hand in the South Atlantic states in 1930 was $409.44, while the earnings in Alabama cotton mills which paid the smallest wages of any Southern state averaged $855.92. See G. T. Schwenning, "Prospects of Southern Textile Unionism," *J. Pol. Econ.*, Dec. 1931.

[11]"It is probable that the widespread adoption of various industrial welfare features has accomplished more toward keeping down the trade union sentiment in southern cotton mill communities than any other one factor" (J. Rhyne, *Some Southern Cotton Mill Workers and Their Villages* [Chapel Hill: University of North Carolina Press, 1930], p. 205). See also B. Mitchell and G. S. Mitchell, *The New Industrial Revolution in the South* (Baltimore: Johns Hopkins Press; London: Oxford University Press, 1930).

[12]See M. Ethridge, "The South's New Industrialism and the Press," *Annals Am. Acad. Pol. Soc. Sci.*, Jan. 1931, pp. 252–253.

International and one gets a picture of some of the obstacles which faced the labor movement when it determined to "go South" in earnest.

At the time, however, it was not so much the indifference of the workers (for the strikes had revealed the presence of long-smoldering grievances ready to burst into flames) as the unfavorable state of public opinion which gave the Federation most cause for worry. To advertise the labor movement as a law-abiding institution, concerned with problems of efficiency and cost reduction, seemed therefore a strategic way of building up a friendlier attitude toward unions. Such a policy commended itself to the Federation on still another ground. If employers should become convinced of the business value of trade unionism, might they not urge their workers to take out union cards? In this way the traditional apathy of the Southern workman toward labor organizations might be broken with the assistance of the employer himself! To determine the extent to which these expectations were fulfilled, we must now trace the progress of the campaign.

Following the Charlotte conference, President Green appointed Paul J. Smith, organizer for the AFL, Francis Gorman, Vice-President of the UTW, and W. C. Birthright, President of the Tennessee Federation of Labor, a committee of three to take charge of the campaign. In addition the Federation engaged a director of educational work, a director of publicity, and an industrial engineer. Southern headquarters were opened at Birmingham, Alabama, and the drive to organize the South got under way.

From the start the work of the campaign fell into two parts. One was the active job of organization by spreading the message of unionism among Southern workers. Educational publicity, dramatics, mass meetings, the distribution of over 600,000 pamphlets — all the usual tools of organizing technique were vigorously plied to acquaint the workers with the meaning of trade unionism.[13] The other part of the program was the advertisement of union-management cooperation through speeches and articles and, most important of all, through the field work of the consulting engineer, Geoffrey Brown, who was retained to approach employers through-

[13] *Convention Proceedings,* 1930, pp. 86–89.

out the South with an explanation of the principles of union-management cooperation as they had been worked out in the Naumkeag sheeting mills of Salem and with an offer of his assistance in putting similar plans into operation in Southern establishments.[14]

In the work of acquainting the public with the constructive purposes of the campaign President Green took the leading role. During the winter of 1930 he made two speaking tours of the major industrial towns of the South, bringing to business men, chambers of commerce, university professors, and state legislatures labor's message of conciliation, good will, and understanding. Union recognition, he pointed out, would mean millions of dollars to the stockholders of Southern industries:

We come preaching the doctrine of cooperation and good will. . . . We are reasonable men and women, reasonable in our outlook on life and reasonable in our conclusions. We know that success to us must come out of success in industry; the greater the earnings of industry the greater the benefits we enjoy. . . . So, standing upon that broad principle we offer to management and to the owners of industry a cooperative organization willing to give the best we have in training and service and skill in order that the industry might be made profitable. . . . We believe that the cooperation of . . . workers who are not smarting under the consciousness that they are denied the exercise of a right will make more money for a mill management than a group of workers who hate the management because it will not let them organize. . . .[15]

While the purposes of the campaign were thus being advertised to the public at large, Geoffrey Brown was bearding the lions in their dens. Between March 1930 and September 1931 he held over 200 conferences with the managers and directors of Southern cotton mills at which he explained the advantages of union-management cooperation and urged the profitableness of union recognition.[16]

I would like to emphasize to you again [he wrote to one manager of a large South Carolina mill following a conference] that the union-management cooperation plan that I am prepared to develop is constructive in character and is designed to place the working force squarely behind production in such a way that a high hourly output per

[14]*Ibid.*, pp. 86–87; *Textile Worker,* March 1930, pp. 745–746.

[15]Green, *Labor Proposes Cooperation,* pp. 10–11 (pamphlet reprint). Cf. *American Federationist,* Feb. 1930, p. 147; July 1930, p. 787; Sept. 1930, pp. 1076–1077.

[16]Correspondence and interviews.

worker, and a minimum unit labor cost will be maintained uniformly throughout the mills. The plan contemplates the organization of a joint cooperative committee to confer at regular intervals on such matters as elimination of unnecessary waste in production; job analysis; orderly planning of work through production; scientific extension (if necessary) of the number of looms, spindles or other equipment per operator; suggestions from workers of a time-saving character; and any other matter in which the effectiveness of the worker influences the prosperity of the mill.

I can state with confidence, and from experience, that the program just outlined can be developed without friction among your workers and that it will give them a new interest in their work. . . . Our union-management cooperative plan, in brief, is the best sort of insurance against possible labor disturbances. . . .[17]

On the whole the results of these conferences were not impressive. Employers displayed an astonishing amount of "sales resistance" to Mr. Brown's "good business proposition." Only three enterprises — all in Columbus, Georgia — agreed to give the plan a trial. Of these, one was a small food packing establishment with 15 or 20 unskilled employees; another was a syrup factory having a total force of 32 Negroes; the third was a hosiery mill employing 30 operatives. In each of these plants it was Brown's offer to place the labor movement of the South squarely behind the sale of the company's products that led the owners to sign a cooperative union agreement copied directly from one in effect at the Naumkeag Mills. The agreement pledged the concern in question to a "cordial and full membership recognition of the bona fide trade union of its employees," whose cooperation was acknowledged as "essential to the continued and successful operation of its manufacturing plant." The union, for its part, agreed to promote the sale of the concern's product and pledged its cooperation in maintaining quantity and quality production and in "effecting such economies in manufacture as may be brought about by the introduction of improved machinery." An optional clause in the agreement, providing for the establishment of a joint research committee to "devise methods of cooperation for the elimination of waste and

[17]Copy in possession of Mr. Brown. See also an article by Brown, "What the Union Offers the South," *American Federationist*, Sept. 1930, pp. 1068–1073.

the improvement of working conditions," was not invoked in any of these cases both because the small size of the plants made such formal machinery unnecessary and because the workers were not deemed sufficiently skilled to be capable of offering practicable suggestions.[18]

Once an agreement had been signed, Brown turned his attention to the matter of sales promotion. Since the products – food and cheap hosiery – were such as to command a wide market among wage earners, arrangements were made to exhibit them before city central labor unions and State Federations of Labor and to distribute the samples to union members throughout the South. As a result of this activity, orders in every case were sufficiently increased to avert wage reductions during the first two years of the depression. All this, of course, was merely an adaptation of the time-honored policy of the union label.

A more novel aspect of Brown's work and one reflecting more concretely the Federation's desire to render "constructive" service to industry was his survey of the hosiery plant in his capacity of consulting engineer. Ever since its organization two years earlier the company had been running with a deficit, unable even when orders increased to make its books balance. By pointing out how the idle time of the machines could be reduced through the provision of an adequate supply of yarn and needles and by suggesting numerous other economies in manufacture, Brown was able to effect savings of several thousands of dollars a year. When all these remedies still left the mill with a deficit, he proposed that the AFL supply funds to increase the capitalization of the plant, thereby enabling it to realize some of the economies of large-scale operation. At this point, however, President Green stopped short. In his opinion the labor movement had done all it could to salvage an unprofitable business from the scrap heap.[19]

But what of the unions which these agreements had brought into

[18]A description of one of these agreements can be found in the *Monthly Labor Review,* April 1931, p. 79. For the information in this and succeeding paragraphs I am indebted to interviews with Mr. Brown and to the opportunity of consulting his files of correspondence.

[19]A partial description of Mr. Brown's work in this plant can be found in the *American Federationist,* Dec. 1931, pp. 1525–1527.

being? Did they represent any genuine conversion to the principles of organization on the part of the operatives, any great addition to the strength of the labor movement?

After Brown and the employer had concluded an agreement, the employees were called together and summarily organized into a union. As Brown put it frankly, "Most of them did not know what it was all about."[20] Nor did they subsequently learn much more. The organizers were too busy promoting the sales of the employer to pay much attention to developing leadership and self-reliance among the newcomers to the union fold. Despite the elaborate phraseology of the agreement, no opportunity was afforded the rank and file to make "constructive contributions" to industrial efficiency. Even the work of sales promotion was carried on without their assistance. They were organizations of little backbone or vitality – hardly the stuff of which a powerful labor movement is fashioned.

Aside from these few unimportant instances, the offer of cooperation won no converts to collective bargaining. The mill owners listened politely to Brown's speeches, informed him that they were perfectly well able to manage their plants without assistance, and ushered him out the door. The Danville situation may be taken as the best illustration of the indifference which union-management cooperation encountered. Early in 1930 the employees of the Dan River and Riverside Cotton Mills in Danville, Virginia, the largest cotton mills in the South, who for eleven years had been organized in a company union modeled after the Leitch plan of Industrial Democracy, were aroused by a 10 percent wage cut to repudiate the whole scheme of Industrial Democracy and to summon organizers from the UTW to help them form a trade union. This gave the AFL an outstanding opportunity to test its new organizing policies. Francis Gorman, Vice-President of the UTW and one of the directors of the Southern organizing campaign, came to Danville to take personal charge of the organizing activities, while Brown

[20]A rather amusing illustration of the naïveté of the workers regarding trade unions was afforded by the election of union officers in one of the plants whose entire force consisted of Negroes. The superintendent, a white man, appeared at the meeting and declared his interest in the organization, whereupon the grateful workers elected him to the vice-presidency of the new local!

went along to sell the cooperative plan to H. R. Fitzgerald, the agent of the mills. Throughout the winter and spring organizing proceeded apace. It was not long before 4,000 members enrolled in the new local. Meanwhile, an avalanche of literature on union-management cooperation, describing the B. and O. Plan and the Naumkeag project of joint research, descended upon Fitzgerald who finally consented to receive the Federation's engineer. To the great disappointment of the union leaders nothing came of the interview. In fact it was rumored that Fitzgerald had been aroused to ire over what he called hypocrisy of the union. He pointed out that, while Brown had been talking of cooperation, some of the union leaders had been calling the mill agent a cradle snatcher as well as other opprobrious epithets which scarcely bespoke a cooperative frame of mind! It was also reported that Fitzgerald had been frightened rather than soothed by the proffer of cooperation, that he had suspected the union of harboring a secret determination to usurp the functions of management once it had gained recognition in the mills!

In vain did the organizers repeat their proffer of cooperation and emphasize their desire to avoid a strike. In vain did President Green come to Danville to speak on labor's interest in productive efficiency and the superiority of union-management cooperation to the company's own plan of "Industrial Democracy." Fitzgerald remained adamant. In the spring and summer the mills began to fire all operatives suspected of union affiliations. By September, with 2000 workers thus dismissed, the newly fledged union was virtually forced to abandon its policy of cooperation and to call a strike.[21] It is not necessary to recount here the long story of the four months' strike which began in September 1930. It is sufficient to point out that, although the Federation threw all its energies into the struggle, it was powerless to cope with injunctions, evictions, troopers, and all the other resources of a management firmly determined to defeat the union no matter what the cost. The Dan-

[21]For a running account of the progress of the Danville campaign see *American Federationist*, April 1930, pp. 402–404, 210–211; June 1930, pp. 658–659; Jan. 1931, p. 19. Also *Textile Worker*, April 1930, p. 51; and *Convention Proceedings*, 1930, p. 210.

ville situation afforded a crucial test of the new organizing technique of the AFL, and at Danville the technique failed.

This leads us to a brief appraisal of the use of union-management cooperation as a device for securing recognition in the South. What were the merits, and what the defects of the policy?

In the first place it is undoubtedly true that Green's speeches went a long way toward dispelling the suspicion and hostility with which the public at large had viewed the entrance of organized labor into the South. A union leader preaching cooperation instead of strife — this was indeed novel to a community accustomed to regard labor organizations as offshoots of the Soviet Republic. Following a talk by Green before 200 business and professional men in Memphis, the *Memphis Commercial Appeal* had this to say:

> William Green, president of the American Federation of Labor, might be taken for the president of a bank, the president of a railroad, a U. S. Senator or a great corporation lawyer.... He is the kind of person who deplores strikes and walkouts and considers friction between employer and employe a result of misunderstanding of economic conditions.... Mr. Green made a favorable impression on those who heard him in Memphis. The policies he advocated might have come with propriety from the president of the American Bankers' Association or the head of any group of business or professional men.[22]

According to Dr. George S. Mitchell, the new cooperative policy of the AFL was responsible for overcoming much of the prejudice against labor organizations in the South. Not only the press but also the churches and the colleges came to view unions in a more favorable light.[23]

But while the public might be won over to the unions' cause by speeches on cooperation, the mill managements refused to be converted. The editor of the leading union-baiting periodical of the South, the *Southern Textile Bulletin,* scornfully labeled the

[22]Quoted in Robert W. Dunn and Jack Hardy, *Labor and Textiles* (New York: International Publishers, 1931), p. 192.

[23]G. S. Mitchell, "Organization of Labor in the South," in *Annals Am. Acad. Pol. and Soc. Sci.,* 153 (Jan. 1931), p. 187. See also his *Textile Unionism and the South,* p. 65. For further comments on the attitude of the public toward the unions see *American Federationist,* March 1930, p. 352; Sept. 1930, p. 1067; and *Convention Proceedings,* 1930, p. 204.

Naumkeag plan a "frame-up" designed to deceive Southern employers as to the real motives of labor organizations. "Where has the American Federation of Labor ever cooperated," he queried, "except temporarily and then only as a means of getting a strangle hold?"[24] In similar vein, the *Textorian,* published by the Cone Mills of Greensboro, North Carolina, printed a statement showing that the losses of the Naumkeag Mills in 1930 had been almost three times as large as those of the Dan River plants. "No additional discussion is necessary," the editor went on, "to show how ridiculous and absurd are the statements of officials, organizers and agitators of the unions relative to what they could accomplish for cotton mills if given a chance."[25] How completely the AFL's talk of cooperation had failed to soothe the apprehensions of Southern mill directors is revealed by the report of the Board of Directors of the Dan River Mills to the stockholders on January 22, 1931. During the past year, it was pointed out, the company had been bothered by labor "agitators and professional propagandists" who had "made their plans to force themselves upon us and obtain control of the labor policies of our Company at any cost." These organizers, the report continued, had brought in speakers "to eulogize the claims of labor and to pour forth upon the public their oft-repeated assurance of fair dealing and of being law-abiding and peaceful. Under the cover thus afforded the most diabolical schemes have been concocted. . . ."[26]

That the labor movement should have been thus thwarted in its attempt to sell itself to management by the promise of cooperation is not surprising, for the salient question which at once arose in the minds of Southern mill owners was simply this: What had the union done at Naumkeag that Southern manufacturers could not as readily accomplish without a union? At the Naumkeag Mills the union had cooperated with the management in introducing the stretch-out system. Under the auspices of an industrial engineer responsible to both the union and the company, the number of looms per weaver had been extended from 12 to 20 over a three

[24]*Southern Textile Bulletin,* July 10, 1930, pp. 20–21. Cf. issue of Jan. 22, 1931, p. 18.

[25]Reprinted in *ibid.,* Feb. 12, 1931, p. 8.

[26]Report of Board of Directors to the Stockholders, Jan. 22, 1931.

year period. But in the South the mill owners had increased the looms from 24 to 48 and 72, overnight. To be sure, in some cases this arbitrary action had been followed by spontaneous walkouts, but a slight downward readjustment in the schedule had usually sufficed to bring the operatives back to the mills. Since the UTW had gone on record as opposed to the introduction of the stretch-out system unless the workers were consulted, it was apparent to the Southern mill owner that so-called union-management co-operation really meant a check upon his ability to reduce costs as he pleased.[27] Moreover, the speeches of some of the organizers condemning the stretch-out system as "vicious" were not likely to put him in a happier frame of mind.[28] The fact that union recognition would eventually result in higher wages and shorter hours – in an end to all the exploitation of "cheap and contented labor" upon which the Southern textile industry relied for its supremacy over the cotton mills of the North – was an additional reason for the manufacturers' refusal to take Green's fine speeches very seriously and for their invariable response of "No interference wanted" to Brown's offers of assistance. Only the smaller plants which were running at a loss or which sold their products to a workers' market were interested in the Federation's proposals. These had everything to gain and nothing to lose from union recognition. But in aiding firms so precariously situated to retrieve their standing the Federation was exposing itself to open attack. The failure of a single plant which had adopted the cooperative program was likely to be pounced upon eagerly by the enemies of the labor movement as a telling example of the perils of collaborating with a union.

More serious, however, than the failure of such a program of conservatism and respectability to appeal to mill executives was its utter lack of those inspirational and dramatic qualities which alone could rally the rank and file about the union banner. If the first act of a new organization should be to reduce the costs of production by increasing the task of the worker – assuming that the proffer of cooperation was made in good faith – would not the

[27]See President McMahon's testimony before the U.S. Senate Committee on Manufactures, *Working Conditions of the Textile Industry*, p. 155; also *Textile Worker*, Sept. 1930, p. 342.

[28]*American Federationist*, Jan. 1930, pp. 37–38.

union appear merely as another agency of exploitation, working hand and glove with the employer? As has been pointed out, the major obstacle to organization in the South was the apathy of the workers. Even the upheavals of 1929 represented not a conversion to union principles but a spontaneous protest against grievances of long standing. To win the rank and file to the union's fold required a policy of militancy rather than respectability, of emphasis on rights rather than on obligations. But given the difficulties which attended the organization of the South at that time and which have continued up to the present, it is only fair to conclude that the use of union-management cooperation as an organizing technique seemed at the time to be worth trying and that its failure was no more spectacular than that of later, more militant campaigns.

CHAPTER VIII

Conclusion: Interpretation of Trade Union Interest in Production

VIEWED in retrospect, union attitudes and policies toward production appear to have undergone a significant modification in the years under survey. From a frankly avowed indifference to problems of production, the AFL shifted its emphasis to advertising the constructive functions of the labor movement in promoting efficiency and eliminating waste. Instead of insisting on the retention of burdensome working rules and regulations, certain individual trade unions showed a readiness to abandon their restrictions and to cooperate with employers in improving shop methods and equipment. While by no means all, nor even a majority, of American trade unions came to acknowledge or assume any responsibility for reducing the costs of production, still the number of organizations participating in cooperative projects of one kind or another was sufficiently large to demand attention.

But at the same time that it was revising its traditional methods along more constructive and conservative lines, the labor movement was passing through a period of inertia and ineptitude. Not only did it make little effort to penetrate the basic industries – steel, automobiles, rubber, food products, chemicals, and electrical equipment. It was also forced by the pressure of new competitive conditions to retreat from such former strongholds as bituminous coal mining and the metal trades until the bulk of union membership was by 1932 concentrated in the sheltered industries and occupations where price competition was lacking or insignificant.[1]

What connection existed between labor's new policy of respectability and its loss of power during the postwar decade? Was union-management cooperation a cause or merely a manifestation of the decline in labor's influence? Or were both the products of more fundamental and deep-seated forces? These questions defy final answers. Some impatient critics of the labor movement attributed the waning strength of the unions not only to their refusal to step outside the boundaries of craft jurisdictions in order to organize the workers engaged in mass production, but also to their reliance on the proffer of cooperation instead of the threat of militancy as a device for winning recognition.[2] In view of the failure of the Southern organizing campaign which was conducted almost exclusively along conservative and respectable lines, some validity might be conceded this observation. But other critics pointed out that the lack of a cooperative policy was at least in part responsible for the decline of the unions in such diverse industries as soft coal mining and upholstery weaving, which were unable to adjust themselves to new competitive conditions because of the inflexibility of union regulations.[3] Support for this interpretation may be found in the fact that, in several instances, unions which were powerless to penetrate open shop regions did manage to protect their position by cooperating with union employers to increase

[1]According to Wolman, 70% of the total union membership in 1930 was represented by the organizations in transportation, building, printing, public service, and theaters (President's Research Committee on Social Trends, *Recent Social Trends in the U.S.* [New York and London: Whittlesey House, McGraw-Hill, 1933] Vol. 2, p. 834). On the other hand, the decline in union membership must not be overestimated. While the total membership of American trade unions in 1931 was 3,298,000 as compared with the high-water mark of 5,110,800 in 1920, it was still considerably above the prewar peak of 2,753,400 reached in 1913 (*ibid.*, p. 832).

For an interesting statistical analysis of the organizing work of the Federation after the war, see L. Stanley, "Collapse of the AFL," *Nation*, Oct. 8, 1930, pp. 367–369.

[2]See, for instance, L. Adamic, "The Collapse of Organized Labor," *Harpers*, Jan. 1933, pp. 167–178; and various articles by J. M. Budish in *Labor Age*, June 1928, p. 8; Nov. 1928, p. 2; Jan. 1929, p. 10; etc.

[3]See J. B. S. Hardman, "How to Break a Union," *New Republic*, Oct. 21, 1931, pp. 252–255; and G. E. Palmer, *Union Tactics and Economic Change* (Philadelphia: University of Pennsylvania Press, 1932).

efficiency and reduce costs. From this point of view, union-management cooperation may also be regarded as a product rather than a cause of union weakness, as a substitute for widespread battles for control, and as a defense of union standards against encroachment. In the last analysis, however, both the policy of cooperation and the impotence of the labor movement were manifestations of the same economic forces and conditions which set the stage for labor action (or inaction) during this period.

Explanation of Trade Union Interest in Production[4]

The primary impetus to trade union interest in production was furnished by the experiences of the labor movement during the First World War. It was the war, it will be remembered,[5] which gave union leaders their first intimate contact with problems of production and industrial management. Through their membership on various government tribunals and labor adjustment boards, which brought them into constant association with technical experts and business executives, they gained a wholly new insight into matters of cost and efficiency, one which had never before entered the range of their vision. By affording this concrete experience in joint industrial control, the war also focused attention on the wider possibilities of industrial democracy. The belief that a new era in industrial relations was at hand, one which held out the promise of labor participation in the management of industry, exerted a profound influence on union thinking both before and after the armistice, persisting even when subsequent events proved this hope to be premature.

A more permanent outcome of the war, however, and one which exerted an even greater influence in directing union thinking into channels of production and efficiency was the reconciliation between scientific management and organized labor, which proceeded further in the years following the war. In view of the bitter hostility

[4]In any attempt to distill out of the compound of influences surrounding a movement those elements which seem to shed most light on its development, there is danger either of omission or of an unwarranted straining of the facts to support a thesis which the writer deems significant. Admitting this possibility of error, the present writer has nevertheless selected for discussion those factors which in her judgment offer the most plausible explanation of trade union interest in production.

[5]For a detailed discussion of these points see Chap. 3, *supra*.

and suspicion which had once characterized the relations between these two groups, the postwar *rapprochement* was significant in paving the way for union experimentation with time study and job analysis – experimentation which would have been impossible had earlier antagonisms persisted. Beside the war, the factors chiefly responsible for this reconciliation were the new emphasis of scientific management on the "human element" in production and the willingness of some of the leading engineers to include the unions in their scheme of industrial relations.

In connection with the influence of scientific management on union policy, the significance of the Federated Engineering Societies' report, *Waste in Industry,* should not be overlooked. It was this survey which led the AFL to urge cooperation between employers and unions in eliminating waste and which helped to shape the new wage theory enunciated by that body in 1925.

While the war focused attention on problems of output and efficiency and the engineers supplied a technique for union-management cooperation, the motives prompting trade union interest in production grew out of certain economic and industrial conditions of the postwar decade which made the task of organized labor more difficult and perplexing than ever before, circumstances which pitted against the unions not only the bitter hostility of the employers but also the indifference of the great mass of workers to the organizers' appeal.[6]

The employers' offensive assumed various shapes. The first few years of the decade saw the organization of a widespread and intensive open shop drive designed to deflate the wartime gains of the unions and to scotch the serpent of radicalism which had reared its head during the strike upheavals of 1919. The toll taken by this offensive is best revealed by the decline in union membership from 5,110,800 in 1920 to 3,592,500 in 1923.[7]

As the fear of labor troubles subsided, the open shop drive gave way to the subtler arts of personnel administration. While the immunization of employees against union propaganda constituted an important objective of personnel policy, the effort to cultivate the

[6]These circumstances have been described in detail in Chap. 4, *supra*.
[7]Wolman, *op. cit.*, p. 119.

good will of the working force was also inspired by the need for making labor more efficient because of the widening gap between money wages and wholesale prices during the decade. With prices declining and money wages advancing, it became necessary to discover other ways of cutting costs by eliminating waste and increasing labor productivity. Hence the spread of employee stock purchase plans, incentive-wage systems, industrial pensions, and shop committees – all designed to create contentment, reduce turnover, and encourage loyalty and efficiency.[8]

More significant, however, than these new labor policies in diminishing the worker's interest in trade unionism and in explaining the consequent failure of the labor movement to push ahead during a period of unprecedented prosperity was the marked rise of per capita real earnings in manufacturing establishments at a rate of 1.4 percent per year from 1922 to 1929.[9] With the increase in wages went a rising standard of consumption, in which the automobile, the movies, and the radio competed with the union for the worker's time and attention.[10]

Beside the new welfare policies and the elevation of living standards there was a third factor which served as a stumbling block to progress in organizing activities. This was the growing rate of industrial displacement, which accompanied the advances in technique and efficiency. A statistical study of the separation rate for wage earners in manufacturing industries shows that during the period 1923 to 1929 one worker out of 20 was each year permanently displaced from the industry in which he worked to seek employment either in another industry or in a nonmanufacturing occupation.[11] Because of this decreasing security of job tenure

[8]For a measurement of the extent to which labor costs in manufacturing industry were reduced from 1923 to 1929, see F. C. Mills, *Economic Tendencies in the United States* (New York: National Bureau of Economic Research, 1932), pp. 409–411.

[9]*Ibid.*, p. 477. It is interesting to note that the real earnings of unskilled factory labor advanced at a more rapid rate than those of skilled labor. The weekly real earnings of the former rose by 2.4% a year as against a 1.6% increase for the latter. Thus, even had the unions been interested in organizing the unskilled, it is doubtful if they could have succeeded in the face of such a sharp rise in real wages.

[10]For an interesting discussion of this point, see Lyle W. Cooper, "American Labor Movement in Prosperity and Depression," *Am. Econ. Rev.*, Dec. 1932, pp. 643–645.

[11]Mills, *op. cit.*, pp. 420–423.

the average worker was unlikely to jeopardize his position for the sake of joining a trade union.

Both the opposition of the employers and the apathy of the workers were thus creating new and troublesome problems for the labor movement, the nature of which has already been described in an earlier chapter. How, in the first place, could the movement appeal to workers who were already satisfied with their wages and conditions of employment? How, in the second place, could employers be persuaded to enter into collective dealings with organized labor when they believed that union recognition was inimical to the interests of productive efficiency? This was the two-horned dilemma which confronted labor leaders in the years following the war. Had the time come for the movement to revise its traditional policies in the light of changing economic conditions, to develop new tactics and methods for solving new problems? That these were the questions agitating the minds of the leaders is indicated by the report of the Executive Council to the 1925 convention of the AFL on "New Economic Developments," which pointed out, "It is useless to continue to use tactics and methods adapted to organization of industry and methods of opposition based upon conditions that existed in previous decades. The unions that make progress against existing difficulties must be able to match brains against brains and information and resourcefulness against information and resourcefulness."[12]

In this effort to devise a new technique and strategy the policy deemed most expedient was that of union-management cooperation. The reason for this decision is not hard to understand, for the difficulties involved both in overcoming the apathy of the workers and in forcing recognition from employers suggested that the easier road to organization lay in selling the union to employers by persuading them that their own self interest could best be promoted through union recognition, that the trade union alone, in contradistinction to the company union or other forms of employee representation, could supply the broad basis of confidence necessary to release the full productive energies of the workers.

[12]*Convention Proceedings,* 1925, p. 33. For a longer excerpt from this report see p. 62, *supra.*

The extent to which this argument was actually successful in overcoming antiunion opposition has already been discussed at length.[13] Here it is only necessary to observe that the same forces which tended to weaken the labor movement were also responsible for the adoption of a policy of conservatism and respectability.

Not only did changing economic conditions determine the use of union-management cooperation as an organizing device by the labor movement as a whole; they also influenced a number of individual unions to experiment with the possibilities of cooperation as a defensive stratagem against nonunion competition in labor costs. The cooperative policies of the Salem Sheeting Workers, the Machinists, the Amalgamated Clothing Workers, and the Full Fashioned Hosiery Workers come readily to mind as illustrations. In fact, the greater number of cooperative ventures were launched in industries or establishments facing new conditions of competition because of technological innovations, the tapping of fresh sources of cheap labor or shifts in demand – changes which took place with an unprecedented suddenness and intensity during the postwar decade. On the other hand, it is equally significant that unions in such sheltered trades as building and railway transportation showed little disposition to modify restrictive working rules or to cooperate with employers in increasing output and eliminating waste.[14] In their case no competitive pressure called for concessions in the interest of industrial efficiency.

Economic change, however, cannot of itself modify union policy. Leadership is necessary to analyze a new industrial situation and to formulate a program for dealing with it. Leadership is also essential in educating the rank and file to acceptance of policies which involve a departure from long established procedures.[15] So far as the AFL is concerned, there is little doubt that William Green was the person chiefly responsible for its support of union-

[13]See Chap. 7, *supra.*

[14]Cf. Haber: "At the present time the attitude of the building trades unions is still largely obstructive. . . . The method is still that of a policeman, a vigilance committee, on the lookout for violators of the standards agreed upon" (*Industrial Relations in the Building Industry* [Cambridge, Mass.: Harvard University Press, 1930], p. 514).

[15]Cf. Hoxie: "Unionism, as a fact, in its constructive aspects is taught to the rank and file by the leaders" (*Trade Unionism in the United States,* p. 177).

management cooperation.[16] An erstwhile Baptist minister, cherishing a belief in the fundamental integrity of all human beings, preferring the conference table to the strike field,[17] Mr. Green consciously molded the Federation after his own conservative and conciliatory image.[18]

In the case of specific experiments in union-management cooperation, the role played by labor leaders was equally significant. In every instance it was the officials who realized that under certain circumstances it was more to labor's advantage to make concessions in the interest of industrial efficiency than to insist on the retention of restrictive working rules and regulations. It was the officials, also, who drew up or helped to frame concrete proposals for reducing costs and who urged their adoption upon the rank and file.

More important than union leadership was the assistance rendered by certain engineers outside the labor movement; they implemented the general policy of cooperation with machinery for joint consultation on all matters involving shop methods and working conditions. To a certain extent the credit for the B. and O. Plan belongs almost exclusively to Captain Otto Beyer, who, as the author of the plan, was also most actively concerned in its development. A similar significance attaches to the services of

[16]It is interesting to speculate in this connection as to whether respectability would have become the shibboleth of the labor movement had Samuel Gompers remained at the helm. While it is true that during the later years of his life, Gompers began to dilute his militancy with the milder waters of cooperation, still his actions at this time could be better accounted for on the grounds of age and weariness, of a natural desire for peace making itself felt after years of turbulent struggle, than on the basis of a fundamental reversal of philosophy. This, at least, was the opinion of Miss Florence Thorne, his secretary, who pointed out that the language of cooperation never came easily to his tongue or pen and who believes that under his stewardship the Federation would never have swung around so completely to the doctrine of respectability (interview, January 1932).

[17]Green, *Modern Trade Unionism,* pp. 13–14.

[18]In a letter to Mr. Geoffrey Brown in 1925 Mr. Green wrote: "In planning for methods of stimulating thought and action in the labor movement...I have been trying to promote the study of constructive problems, and have been thinking over the possibility of asking a number of progressive industrial engineers to discuss in very simple nontechnical language how unions can enter upon cooperative undertakings with management for the development of more efficient practices and processes" (copy in possession of Mr. Brown). Numerous articles of this kind subsequently made their appearance in the *Federationist.*

Morris L. Cooke and Francis Goodell in building up a technique for union participation in job analysis.

Not one, but many factors thus explain the growth of trade union interest in production: the war, the reconciliation between scientific management and organized labor, changing economic and industrial conditions, union leadership, the services of engineers — all must be included in any cogent interpretation of the new trends in union attitudes and policies toward output. The significance of these policies will be reviewed in the next and final section.

Significance of Trade Union Interest in Production

In appraising the significance of trade union interest in production from the point of view of union strategy and outlook, several questions arise. What, for example, was the utility of cooperation as an organizing device, as a method for protecting union standards? How did it affect jobs, wages, and working conditions? What were the implications of the policy so far as the objectives of the labor movement were concerned? Did it represent a step toward ultimate workers' control of industry?

Turning first to the use of union-management cooperation as an organizing device, we note that almost every attempt to secure recognition through the proffer of cooperation ended in failure. The Southern organizing campaign of the AFL affords the best illustration of the complete futility of this type of appeal. Nor is the reason far to seek. No amount of persuasion based on the "cash value" of the union made the slightest impression on employers who were strongly hostile to the labor movement and who were furthermore convinced that all talk of "cooperation" was merely a veil to conceal the real objectives of the movement, namely, higher wages, shorter hours, and interference with managerial prerogatives. Experience demonstrated that it was only the small establishment running at a loss and unable to afford technical assistance that would sign a collective agreement in order to secure the services of the union's technicians in reducing costs or to avail itself of the union's efforts in expanding sales.

More serious, however, than the failure of such a policy to soften the opposition of employers was its utter lack of those dramatic and inspirational qualities which alone could rally the rank and file about the union banner. In view of the fact that the apathy of the workers was one of the most serious problems confronting the labor movement at that time, it is not difficult to understand how emphasis upon cooperation, upon the obligations rather than the rights of the workers, could fail to win many converts to the union fold. If the first act of a newly fledged union should be to reduce costs by sanctioning an increase in tasks, would not the union appear to be more concerned for the profits of the employer than for the welfare of the workers? And if this were the case, how long could it command the allegiance of the rank and file?

Sooner or later unions which experimented with cooperation as an organizing technique reverted to more militant tactics. A new militant note was sounded at the 1932 convention of the AFL, when, in what was termed "the greatest fighting speech of his career," President Green declared that labor's patience with management was at an end, that henceforth the movement must revert to "forceful methods" to secure its objectives, chief among which was the shorter week.[19] The declaration is significant in indicating the close of an era of conscious conservatism and respectability.[20]

While the policy of union-management cooperation had little to commend it as an organizing device, there was more to be said for it as a defensive stratagem in protecting union shops from nonunion competition in labor costs. On occasions when organized employers were facing severe competition, it was obviously wiser for the union to assist them in reducing costs than to stand back and allow them to be driven into the nonunion field or forced into liquidation. Such assistance often took the form of removing restrictions on output, of utilizing the technical skill of trained busi-

[19] *New York Times,* Nov. 29, 1932.

[20] That this speech marked a definite break with tradition is revealed by a leading editorial in the *New York Times,* titled "Not a Time to Quarrel," which began: "Surprise and disappointment will be caused by the speech of President Green at the convention of the American Federation of Labor at Cincinnati. He has been reckoned among the most steadygoing and reasonable labor leaders. His position as head of a powerful organization is one of great influence, and this he has always seemed to desire to use in a spirit of moderation and with a proper sense of responsibility" (*New York Times,* Nov. 30, 1932).

ness agents in reorganizing shop methods and equipment, and even of hiring outside engineers to perform similar services. Unions which at the time molded their policies along these lines included the Pressmen, the Salem Sheeting Workers, the Machinists, and, most important of all, the Amalgamated Clothing Workers.

From the point of view of the union, the purpose of these activities was to entrench its position more firmly, to preserve the jobs of its members, and, if possible, to defer a reduction in wages by discovering other methods of cutting costs. Through loans and technical assistance to manufacturers hovering on the brink of in solvency, the Amalgamated Clothing Workers saved the jobs of thousands of workers who otherwise would have been thrown upon the streets by the bankruptcy of their employers. Even though a curtailment of the Naumkeag working force was ultimately required by changes in equipment and methods, still, through a program of joint research, the Salem Sheeting Workers did, to a degree, control the rate of technological change in the interest of its members. And while a wage reduction was in the end unavoidable, still, it was deferred for a number of years by eliminating waste and increasing production. In the last analysis, however, only a further extension of union control could enable a labor organization to maintain its standards of wages and hours substantially above nonunion levels in time of depression. Thus while union engineering and joint research possessed significance as temporary expedients for helping an individual employer to survive an emergency, they were not methods generally or continuously employed by any one union over a period of time.

A final question concerns the implications of trade union interest in production with reference to the general philosophy and basic objectives of the labor movement. Did union-management cooperation imply a wholesale acceptance of the capitalist system or did it represent a step toward ultimate workers' control of industry?

According to some of the more radical critics of the labor movement, the policy of union-management cooperation was to be condemned as an abject surrender to capitalism, as a form of class collaboration based on the belief that "a labor union has more common interest with the employers of their own industry than with the workers of all the other industries."[21] The dangers of such an attitude were painted in alarming colors by Mr. A. J. Muste, the editor of *Labor Age:*

A union which consciously or unconsciously comes to think of itself as an agency to help the employer to get efficient production very soon will cease to be a genuine union. If the union keeps its primary purpose of protecting and advancing the interests of the workers foremost, almost any compromise may be temporarily justified; if the union has the attitude that it is a personnel agency for the boss, even the smallest compromise is a step on the road to ruin and the betrayal of the workers.[22]

A similar interpretation but a different judgment was given by Professor Commons:

The rise of revolutionary unionism in the United States has forced the regular unions of the American Federation of Labor and the railroad brotherhoods into a position of frankly protecting and standing up for the capitalist system and they are today the greatest bulwark which employers have against these revolutionary unions. Furthermore this situation has led these conservative unions to take the employers' point of view in increasing efficiency, extending markets and helping the development of productivity. In general the tendency of unionism, when once the employer has recognized it and dealt with it on an equality is to give up revolutionary ideas of overthrowing capitalism and adopt partnership ideas with the employer.[23]

An entirely different interpretation was offered by some students and members of the labor movement who maintained that far

[21]*Labor Age,* June 1928, p. 8.

[22]*Ibid.,* July 1931, p. 9. This is only one of a large number of articles and editorials, all carrying the same refrain of "class collaboration." Cartoons were likewise used to ridicule the policy of union engineering. For example, a cartoon entitled "A Tale of Ten Years" appeared in the issue for September 1930. The upper portion, representing "Labor Day, 1920," showed a worker, in response to a notice of a 10% wage cut, threatening the Boss: "If you do we'll strike your plant." The lower portion, "Labor Day, 1930," depicted a cringing labor official pleading in answer to a similar notice: "Please don't cut wages, if you don't I'll install our famous efficiency system, I'll make my men do more work. Anything. Please Mister Boss don't cut wages!"

[23]*Interborough Rapid Transit Company* v. *William Green, et al.: Brief for Defendants,* p. 422. It must be remembered, however, that this statement was designed to commend the unions to the court.

from strengthening the foundations of capitalism, union-management cooperation constituted an implicit challenge to the whole system. From this point of view trade unions which took an interest in problems of cost and production were acquiring a background of technical knowledge and competence in preparation for a coming era of workers' control of industry. Moreover, by proving their indispensability so far as the efficient conduct of industry was concerned, labor organizations were steadily accumulating the power necessary to overthrow the capitalist system. Such at least was one explanation of the constructive policies of the Amalgamated Clothing Workers.[24]

Yet neither class collaboration nor class consciousness affords an adequate interpretation of trade union interest in production. So far as the AFL and its constituents were concerned, larger visions of a new social order served as a minor stimulus to union action, for the labor movement was still, as it was in the early days, pursuing an opportunistic course with scant reference to "ultimate ends" of any sort. Nor was it primarily a consideration of the needs of industry which prompted the labor movement to develop a philosophy of union-management cooperation. Union attitudes and policies toward production had a more pragmatic flavoring than either of the above interpretations would suggest. In brief they were concerned with neither the preservation nor the destruction of the capitalist system, but with interests which more immediately touched the lives of union members: job opportunities, wages, and working conditions. Only in the stronger emphasis on the democratic rights of workers to a voice in the shaping of these conditions and on the responsibilities of labor to promote efficiency did the new doctrines add to the old formulae. As such they served to broaden the outlook of the labor movement and to aid the adjustment which both unions and management had to make if industrial democracy were to be achieved.

[24]See, for example, J. M. Budish, and George Soule, *The New Unionism in the Clothing Industry* (New York: Harcourt Brace, 1920).

Epilogue

FROM the perspective of the two decades which have elapsed what significance can we attribute to the growth of trade union interest in production during the 1920's? Was this interest a mere flash in the pan, or at best a campaign which must be written off as another "Noble Experiment"? To those who were writing at the time (the present author included) the whole movement seemed to have failed to achieve the goals which it sought. The new problems and developments of succeeding decades again changed both the environment and strategy of organized labor, threatening to submerge the interest in cooperation. With the growth of more favorable labor legislation in the thirties and the organization of the CIO came a renewed emphasis on militancy rather than on cooperation as an organizing technique. Moreover, the pressures of the depression caused the downfall of many of the promising experiments in union-management cooperation, while the fear of unemployment made it impolitic for union leaders to stress the need for increasing efficiency.

It was not until the Second World War that a revival of interest in production committees occurred, again, as during the First World War, under government sponsorship. With the passing of the emergency most of these ventures likewise disappeared. But, when a wave of postwar strikes once more created an atmosphere hostile to the labor movement, which soon took the form of restrictive labor legislation, the labor movement again felt called upon to demonstrate its capacity for responsible industrial citizenship, this time by sponsoring case studies of industrial peace.[1]

It is here that we can go back and pick up a thread linking the earlier movement to the present. For Morris L. Cooke who had played such an influential role in the early developments continued to exert his influence, this time on the newly organized CIO. It was Cooke who collaborated with Philip Murray on the volume, *Organized Labor and Production,* which is an excellent restatement of the philosophy of the twenties. In fact the Steelworkers became the heirs of the tradition, expounding in such works as Golden and Ruttenberg's *Dynamics of Industrial Democracy* the theme that union-management cooperation would follow union recognition and security. Another staff member of the Steelworkers, Joseph Scanlon, sought to advance in practice the ideas expressed in these volumes. It is also interesting to note that such union leaders as Golden and Scanlon demonstrated the reconciliation which Gompers and Green had begun, by themselves joining the ranks of the intellectuals. Their university connections gave them a base from which to promote further experiments in union-management cooperation as well as to stimulate the case studies of industrial peace referred to above. In fact their interest in production expanded beyond the stage of stressing formal plans of cooperation to a recognition of the many variables involved in "constructive" labor relations – the keynote of the new philosophy. Labor's interest in national production goals as voiced by Walter Reuther carried forward the ideas expressed by Gompers in the twenties, while the "improvement factor" in wage adjustments served as a concrete means of expressing the "New Wage Philosophy" of the earlier period.

Thus it can be seen that the trend which Gompers and Green set in motion has continued, with sensitive adaptations to the times. The labor movement has come a long way from its early denial of any concern with industrial efficiency. The experiments of the twenties, tentative and inconclusive as they were, can be seen as part of the long process of adjustment by which organized labor has sought to meet the challenge of a changing environment.

[1]See National Planning Association case studies published under the title, *Causes of Industrial Peace* (Washington, D.C.: NPA, Sept. 1948 –).

Bibliography

MUCH of the manuscript material used in this study consisted of correspondence and miscellaneous memoranda which do not lend themselves to formal classification and which are not easily accessible. For this reason, only the more available sources have been included in the bibliography. Because of the extensive territory covered, it has seemed desirable to classify the secondary references according to subject matter. To avoid unnecessary duplication, only the most important articles and pamphlets are cited; complete reference to the others may be found in the footnotes. To aid those who may wish contemporary material on the specific experiments in union-management cooperation, I have included the references used in the unpublished portion of the study.

A. BIBLIOGRAPHIES AND YEAR BOOKS

Amalgamated Clothing Workers. *Bibliography of Source Material, Articles, and Books on the Amalgamated Clothing Workers of America.* New York: May 1929. (Pamphlet.)

Rand School of Social Science. *American Labor Year Book.* New York: Rand School of Social Science, 1919–1932.

U.S. Bureau of Labor Statistics. "Union-Management Cooperation: A List of References." Compiled by Laura A. Thompson. *Monthly Labor Review,* October 1927, pp. 220–227.

B. ORIGINAL SOURCES

1. *Cooperative Agreements and Reports on Cooperative Projects*

Baltimore and Ohio Railroad

"Memorandum Agreement between the Federated Shop Crafts and the Baltimore and Ohio Railroad: Effective March 5, 1925." Unpublished ms., 1925.

Brotherhood of Railway Clerks

Oliver, E. L. "Possibilities of Co-operation between the Management of the Grand Trunk Railway and the Brotherhood of Railway Clerks." Unpublished ms., 1931.

"Report of Fact Finding Committee, Car Service Department, Baltimore and Ohio Railroad." Unpublished ms., April 30, 1927.

Canadian National Railways

Beyer, Otto S. "Discussion of System of Payment by Results Formerly in Effect in the Shops of the Canadian National Railways." Unpublished ms., August 23, 1924.

———. "Report Covering the Development of Union-Management Cooperation in the Maintenance of Equipment Service of the Canadian National Railways." Unpublished ms., August 23, 1924.

———. "Union-Management Cooperative Program, Maintenance of Way Service, Canadian National Railways." Unpublished ms., April 3, 1932.

Black, R. A. "Report on the Education of Maintenance of Way Employees." Unpublished ms., September 10, 1931.

Cleveland Garment Industry

Goodell, F. *A Report on the Production Standards Situation in the Ladies' Garment Industry of Cleveland.* August 1925. (Mimeographed and bound.)

Oliver, E. L. "Functioning of the Joint Bureau of Standards." Unpublished ms., October 1, 1923.

Naumkeag Steam Cotton Company

"Agreement between United Textile Workers and Naumkeag Steam Cotton Company." Unpublished ms., April 1927.

"Information on Displacement by Machines and Methods." Unpublished ms., September 18, 1931.

"Three Years with Joint Research." Unpublished ms., January 14, 1932.

St. Louis Public Service Company

"Memorandum of Cooperative Agreement with Division No. 788, Amalgamated Association of Street and Electric Railway Employees." Unpublished ms., September 16, 1930.

2. *Arbitration Cases*

Amalgamated Clothing Workers

Mens Clothing Industry, Chicago Market. *Decisions of the Board of Arbitration: Direct and Appealed.* 1919–1925. (Mimeographed and bound.)

"Miscellaneous Decisions of Baltimore, Rochester and New York Trade Boards." Unpublished ms., 1919–1931.

American Federation of Labor

Oliphant, H. *Interborough Rapid Transit Company against William Green, et al.: Brief for Defendants.* New York: Workers Education Bureau, 1928.

Railway Employes' Department. *The Case of the Railway Shopmen.* Chicago: Railway Employes' Department, 1922.

Baltimore and Ohio Railroad

Labor Bureau, Inc. "Data for Negotiations for System Federation No. 30, Baltimore and Ohio Railroad." Unpublished ms., April 12, 1923.

———. "Memorandum on Wage Increase and Overtime Payment for System Federation No. 30, Baltimore and Ohio Railroad." Unpublished ms., April 1925.

Cleveland Garment Industry

Labor Bureau, Inc. "Brief for the Union on Wages in Arbitration Proceedings between Cleveland Joint Board, Ladies' Garment Workers' Union and Cleveland Garment Manufacturers' Association." Unpublished ms., April 21, 1923; June 5, 1926.

Electrical Construction Industry

Council on Industrial Relations. *Bulletins of Decisions.* March 15, 1921–October 2, 1930.

Full Fashioned Hosiery Industry

"Decisions of the Impartial Chairman." Series E. Unpublished ms., September 1931–1932.

Naumkeag Steam Cotton Company

Labor Bureau, Inc. "Material for Wage Negotiations with the Naumkeag Steam Cotton Company of Salem, Mass. Prepared for Sheeting Workers' Local No. 33." Unpublished ms., January 1925; February 1928.

Schweinler Press Arbitration Case

New York Employing Printers' Association, Printers' League Section. "Briefs for Arbitration and Rebuttal." Unpublished ms., July 28, 1930.

New York Printing Press Assistants' Union No. 23. "Briefs for Arbitration and Rebuttal." Unpublished ms., July 28, 1930.

"Majority Opinion." Unpublished ms., August 14, 1930.

"Minority Opinion." Unpublished ms., August 14, 1930.

3. *Trade Union Documents*

Amalgamated Association of Street and Electric Railway Employees

Motorman and Conductor. 1927–1931.

Amalgamated Clothing Workers of America

The Advance. 1920–1932.

Documentary History. 1914–1930.

Hart, Schaffner and Marx Labor Agreement. Edited by Earl Dean Howard. 1920. (Pamphlet.)

American Federation of Full Fashioned Hosiery Workers

Convention Proceedings. 1929–1931. (Transcript.)

"National Agreement with Full Fashioned Hosiery Manufacturers of America." Unpublished ms., 1929.

National Agreement and Uniform Price Scale. 1931–1932. (Pamphlet.)

American Federation of Labor

American Federationist. 1894–1932.

Report of Proceedings of the...Annual Convention of the American Federation of Labor. 1886–1931.

Brotherhood of Maintenance of Way Employes

Convention Proceedings. 1925, 1928.

Report of the Grand Lodge President. September 14, 1931.

Brotherhood of Painters, Decorators and Paperhangers of America

Painter and Decorator. 1927–1931.

Brotherhood of Sleeping Car Porters

The Black Worker. December 1, 1929–September 1, 1930.

Cigar Makers' International Union

Constitution. 1920, 1923.

"Convention Proceedings," *Cigar Makers' Journal,* September, 1923–1929.

International Association of Machinists

Convention Proceedings. 1924, 1928.

International Brotherhood of Electrical Workers

Agreement between the Electrical Guild of North America

and the International Brotherhood of Electrical Workers. September 15, 1931.
Constitution of the Council on Industrial Relations for the Electrical Construction Industry. March 30, 1931.
Journal of Electrical Workers and Operators. 1928–1931.
International Ladies' Garment Workers' Union
Convention Proceedings. 1916–1928.
Justice. 1919–1931.
The Ladies' Garment Worker. 1912–1919.
International Printing Pressmen and Assistants' Union
The American Pressman. 1924–1931.
Order of Sleeping Car Conductors
The Sleeping Car Conductor. 1927–1931.
Railway Employes' Department, American Federation of Labor
Constitution and By-Laws. 1930.
Convention Proceedings. 1920–1930.
Baltimore and Ohio System Federation No. 30. *Daily Minutes of the Convention.* 1923–1930.
Canadian National System Federation No. 11. *Convention Proceedings.* 1926–1930.
Division No. 4. *Convention Proceedings.* 1924–1928.
United Mine Workers, District No. 15
Agreement with the Rocky Mountain Fuel Company. September 1, 1928–August 31, 1930; September 1, 1930–August 31, 1932.
United Textile Workers
Convention Proceedings. 1928.
The Textile Worker. 1921–1931.
Local No. 33, *Agreement, Rules and By-Laws.* 1930.

4. *Government Documents*

U.S., Commission on Industrial Relations of 1912. *Final Report and Testimony.* 11 vols. Washington, D.C.: Government Printing Office, 1916.
U.S., Eleventh Special Report of the Commissioner of Labor. *Regulation and Restriction of Output.* Washington, D.C.: Government Printing Office, 1904.
U.S., Industrial Commission of 1898. *Report.* 19 vols. Washington, D.C.: Government Printing Office, 1902.

U.S. Senate. Committee on Education and Labor Investigating Strike in Steel Industries. *Report.* Washington, D.C.: Government Printing Office, 1919.

U.S. Senate. Committee on Manufactures. *Working Conditions in the Textile Industry in North Carolina, South Carolina and Tennessee: Hearings, May 8, 9, 20, 1929.* Washington, D. C.: Government Printing Office, 1929.

C. SECONDARY SOURCES

1. *General References*

Adamic, Louis. *Dynamite: The Story of Class Violence in America.* New York: Viking Press, 1931.

Barker, J. E. *America's Secret.* London: Murray, 1927.

Barnett, George E. *Chapters on Machinery and Labor.* Cambridge, Mass.: Harvard University Press, 1926.

———. *The Printers.* (Publications of the American Economic Association, Ser. 3, Vol. 10.) Washington, D. C.: 1909.

Bimba, Anthony. *The History of the American Working Class.* New York: International Publishers, 1927.

Butler, H. B. *Industrial Relations in the United States.* Geneva: International Labour Office, 1927.

Catlin, Warren B. *The Labor Problem in the United States and Great Britain.* New York: Harper, 1926.

Commons, John R. *History of Labor in the United States.* 2 vols. New York: Macmillan, 1921.

———. "Organized Labor's Attitude toward Industrial Efficiency," *American Economic Review,* Sept. 1911, pp. 463–472.

———. "Restrictions by Trade Unions," *Outlook,* Oct. 1906, pp. 470–476.

Cooke, Morris L., Gompers, S., and Miller, Fred J. (eds.). "Labor, Management and Production," *Annals of the American Academy of Political and Social Science,* 91 (1920).

"Cooperation of Trade-Unions with Employers," *Monthly Labor Review,* Oct. 1928, pp. 657–679.

Council of Ruskin College. *The Trade Unions and Output.* Birmingham, England: Birmingham Printers, 1920.

Daily Mail Trade Union Mission to the United States. 1927. (Pamphlet.)

Douglas, Paul H., and Director, Aaron. *The Problem of Unemployment.* New York: Macmillan, 1931.

Dubreuil, H. *Robots or Men?* New York: Harper, 1930.

Gemmill, Paul F. *Present-Day Labor Relations.* New York: John Wiley, 1929.

Gluck, Elsie. *John Mitchell, Miner.* New York: John Day, 1929.

Gompers, Samuel. *The American Labor Movement, Its Make-up, Achievements and Aspirations.* 1914. (Pamphlet.)

———. *Labor and the Employer.* New York: Dutton, 1920.

———. *Seventy Years of Life and Labor.* 2 vols. New York: Dutton, 1925.

Great Britain. *Report of the Delegation Appointed to Study Industrial Conditions in Canada and the United States of America.* London: His Majesty's Stationery Office, 1927.

Green, William. *Labor Proposes Cooperation.* 1930. (Pamphlet.)

———. *Modern Trade Unionism.* 1925. (Pamphlet.)

———. "Recent Trends in the Organized Labor Movement," *Annals of the American Academy of Political and Social Science,* May 1930, pp. 183–191.

Haber, William. *Industrial Relations in the Building Industry.* Cambridge, Mass.: Harvard University Press, 1930.

Hardman, J. B. S. *American Labor Dynamics.* New York: Harcourt Brace, 1928.

Helbing, Albert T. *The Departments of the American Federation of Labor.* Baltimore: Johns Hopkins University, 1931.

Hoxie, Robert F. *Trade Unionism in the United States.* New York: Appleton, 1924.

The Industrial Future of New England: Proceedings of the First New England Labor Congress Held in Worcester, Massachusetts, October 25–27, 1929. New York: Workers Education Bureau Press, 1929.

International Association for the Study and Improvement of Human Relations and Conditions in Industry. *Report of the First Triennial Congress Held at Cambridge (England), July 1928 on the Subject of Fundamental Relationships between All Sections of the Industrial Community.* 2 vols. The Hague, 1928.

Lewisohn, S. A., and Moon, P. T. (eds.). "Constructive Experiments in Industrial Cooperation between Employers and

Employees," *Proceedings, Academy of Political Science,* Vol. 9, No. 4 (1922).

Mathewson, Stanley B. *Restriction of Output among Unorganized Workers.* New York: Viking Press, 1931.

Mills, F. C. *Economic Tendencies in the United States.* New York: National Bureau of Economic Research, 1932.

Mitchell, John. *Organized Labor.* Philadelphia: American Book and Bible House, 1903.

Montgomery, Royal E. *Industrial Relations in the Chicago Building Trades.* Chicago: University of Chicago Press, 1927.

Muir, Ramsay. *America the Golden.* London: Williams and Norgate, 1927.

National Bureau of Economic Research. *Recent Economic Changes in the United States.* 2 vols. New York: McGraw-Hill, 1929.

Palmer, Gladys L. *Union Tactics and Economic Change.* Philadelphia: University of Pennsylvania Press, 1932.

Perlman, Selig. *A History of Trade Unionism in the United States.* New York: Macmillan, 1922.

———. *A Theory of the Labor Movement.* New York: Macmillan, 1928.

President's Research Committee on Social Trends. *Recent Social Trends in the United States.* 2 vols. New York: McGraw-Hill, 1933.

Proceedings of Conference on New Relations between Labor and Capital, Arranged by Philadelphia Labor College, February 2 and 3, 1939. (Pamphlet.)

Reed, Louis S. *The Labor Philosophy of Samuel Gompers.* (Columbia University Studies in History, Economics and Public Law, No. 327.) New York: Columbia University Press, 1930.

Slichter, Sumner H. *Modern Economic Society.* New York: Holt, 1931.

Stewart, Bryce M. *Unemployment Benefits in the United States.* New York: Industrial Relations Counselors, 1930.

Tippett, Tom. *When Southern Labor Stirs.* New York: Cape and Smith, 1931.

Tugwell, Rexford G. *Industry's Coming of Age.* New York: Harcourt Brace, 1927.

Walling, William E. *American Labor and American Democracy*. New York: Harper, 1926.

Webb, Sidney, and Webb, Beatrice. *Industrial Democracy*. New York: Longmans, Green, 1919.

Wertheim Lectures on Industrial Relations, 1928. Cambridge, Mass.: Harvard University Press, 1929.

Wolman, Leo. *The Growth of American Trade Unions: 1880–1923*. New York: National Bureau of Economic Research, 1924.

2. *Wage Theories of Organized Labor*

American Federation of Labor. *Organized Labor's Modern Wage Policy*. 1927. (Pamphlet.)

———. *Wages and Labor's Share*. By J. Kucznski and M. Steinfeld. 1927. (Pamphlet.)

———. Railway Employes' Department. *The Problem of Piece Work*. Chicago: Bronson Canode, 1921.

Cole, G. D. H. *The Payment of Wages*. London: Allen and Unwin, 1918.

Cooper, Lyle W. "The American Federation of Labor and the Intellectuals," *Political Science Quarterly*, Sept. 1928, pp. 387–407.

Douglas, Paul. *Real Wages in the United States, 1890–1926*. New York: Houghton Mifflin, 1930.

Feis, Herbert (ed.). *Principles of Wage Settlement*. New York: Wilson, 1924.

Gompers, Samuel. *The Eight-Hour Workday: Its Inauguration, Enforcement and Influences*. Washington, D.C.: AFL, 1906.

Green, William. *Wage Theories*. 1926. (Pamphlet.)

Gunton, George. *The Social and Economic Importance of the Eight Hour Movement*. Washington, D.C.: AFL, 1889.

Hamilton, Walton, and May, Stacy. *The Control of Wages*. New York: Doran, 1923.

Lauck, William J. *The New Industrial Revolution and Wages*. New York: Funk and Wagnalls, 1929.

Laughlin, James L. *Latter-Day Problems*. New York: Scribners, 1909.

———. *Tracts for the Times: Labor and Wages*. Washington, D.C.: W. F. Roberts, 1920.

———. "The Unions versus Higher Wages," *Journal of Political Economy,* March 1906, pp. 129–142.

McCabe, David A. *The Standard Rate in American Trade Unions.* Baltimore: Johns Hopkins University Press, 1912.

McNeill, George E. *The Eight-Hour Primer: The Fact, Theory and Argument.* 1889. (Pamphlet.)

Mussey, Henry R. "Eight-Hour Theory in the American Federation of Labor," in *Economic Essays Contributed in Honor of John Bates Clark,* ed. J. H. Hollander. New York: Macmillan, 1927.

National Industrial Conference Board. *Systems of Wage Payment.* New York: 1930.

National Metal Trades Association. *Methods of Wage Payment.* Chicago: 1928.

Steward, Ira. *The Eight-Hour Movement: A Reduction of Hours Is an Increase of Wages.* 1865. (Pamphlet.)

"Wage Policy of the American Federation of Labor," *Monthly Labor Review,* Oct. 1927, pp. 845–850.

3. *Organized Labor and the War*

American Federation of Labor. *Labor and the War.* Washington, D.C.: AFL, 1918.

Barnett, George E. "American Trade Unionism and the Standardization of Wages during the War," *Journal of Political Economy,* Oct. 1919, pp. 670–693.

Garton Foundation. *Memorandum on the Industrial Situation after the War.* London: Harrison, 1916.

Hines, Walker D. *War History of American Railroads.* New Haven: Yale University Press, 1928.

Hotchkiss, Willard E., and Seager, Henry R. *History of the Shipbuilding Labor Adjustment Board: 1917–1919.* (Bulletin of the Bureau of Labor Statistics, No. 283.) Washington, D.C.: Government Printing Office, 1921.

National War Labor Board. (Bulletin of the Bureau of Labor Statistics, No. 287.) Washington, D. C.: Government Printing Office, 1922.

Sprague, O. M. "Relations between Labor and Capital and Reconstruction," *American Economic Review,* Dec. 1918, pp. 763–773.

Watkins, Gordon S. *Labor Problems and Labor Administration in the United States during the World War.* (University of Illinois Studies in the Social Sciences, Vol. 8, Nos. 3, 4, Sept. 1919 and Dec. 1919.) Urbana: University of Illinois, 1919.

Wehle, Louis B. "War Labor Policies and the Outcome in Peace," *Quarterly Journal of Economics*, Feb. 1919, pp. 321–343.

Whitley Committee. *The Industrial Council Plan in Great Britain*. Washington, D. C.: Bureau of Industrial Research, 1919.

Wolfe, A. B. *Works Committees and Joint Industrial Councils*. Philadelphia: U.S. Shipping Board, 1919.

4. *Organized Labor and Scientific Management*

Brandeis, Louis. "Organized Labor and Efficiency," *Survey*, April 1911, pp. 150–151.

———. *Scientific Management and the Railroads*. New York: Engineering Magazine, 1911.

Brown, Geoffrey C. "Workers' Participation in Job Study," *Bulletin of the Taylor Society*, June 1927, pp. 414–420.

Bulletin of the Taylor Society. 1916–1932.

Cooke, Morris L. "Some Observations on Workers' Organizations," *Bulletin of the Taylor Society*, Feb. 1929, pp. 2–10.

Copley, Frank B. *Frederick Winslow Taylor*. 2 vols. New York: Harper, 1923.

Devinat, Paul. "The American Labor Movement and Scientific Management," *International Labor Review*, April 1926, pp. 461–468.

Drury, Horace B. *Scientific Management*. (Columbia University Studies in History, Economics and Public Law, Vol. 65.) New York: Columbia University Press, 1915.

Federated Engineering Societies. *Waste in Industry*. New York: McGraw-Hill, 1921.

Green, William. "Labor's Ideals Concerning Management," *Bulletin of the Taylor Society*, Dec. 1925, pp. 242–246.

Hoxie, Robert F. *Scientific Management and Labor*. New York: Appleton, 1915.

Hunt, Edward Eyre. *Scientific Management since Taylor*. New York: Harper, 1923. (First ed., 1911.)

Person, Harlow S. (ed.). *Scientific Management in American Industry*. New York: Harper, 1929.

Taylor, Frederick W. "A Piece Rate System," *Economic Studies of the American Economic Association,* 1 (June 1886), 89–129.

———. *The Principles of Scientific Management.* 2d ed. New York: Harper, 1923. (First ed., 1911.)

———. "Scientific Management and Labor Unions," *Bulletin of the Society to Promote the Science of Management,* Dec. 1914.

5. *The Postwar Industrial Offensive*

Berman, Edward. *Labor and the Sherman Act.* New York: Harper, 1930.

Bonnett, Clarence E. *Employers' Associations in the United States.* New York: Macmillan, 1922.

Burton, Ernest R. *Employee Representation.* Baltimore: Williams and Wilkins, 1926.

Commission of Inquiry, Interchurch World Movement. *Report on the Steel Strike of 1919.* New York: Harcourt Brace, 1920.

Cooper, Lyle W. "Organized Labor and the Trust," *Journal of Political Economy,* Dec. 1928, pp. 720–740.

Dickinson, Z. C. *Suggestions from Employees.* (Michigan Business Studies, Vol. 1, No. 8, August 1927.) Ann Arbor: University of Michigan, 1927.

Donald, W. J., and Donald, E. K. "Trends in Personnel Administration," *Harvard Business Review,* Jan. 1929, pp. 143–155.

Dunn, Robert W. *Company Unions.* New York: Vanguard, 1927.

———. *The Americanization of Labor.* New York: International Publishers, 1927.

Employee Representation or Works Councils. Washington, D.C.: Chamber of Commerce of the United States, 1927. (Pamphlet.)

French, Carroll E. *The Shop Committee in the United States.* (Johns Hopkins Studies in Historical and Political Science, Ser. 41, No. 2) Baltimore: Johns Hopkins University Press, 1923.

Frankfurter, Felix, and Greene, Nathan. *The Labor Injunction.* New York: Macmillan, 1930.

Gompers, Samuel. *Correspondence with Newton D. Baker.* 1923. (Pamphlet.)

———. *The Fundamental Issues: Present Industrial Controversies an Expression of Vital Conflict between Industry and Finance.* New York: 1922. (Reprinted from *New York Times,* July 23, 1922.)

Miller, Earl J. *Workmen's Representation in Industrial Government.* (University of Illinois Studies in the Social Sciences, Vol. 10, Nos. 3, 4, September–December, 1922.) Urbana: University of Illinois, 1922.

National Industrial Conference Board. *Experience with Works Councils in the United States.* (Research Report No. 50.) New York: National Industrial Conference Board, 1922.

———. *Industrial Relations Programs in Small Plants.* New York: National Industrial Conference Board, 1921.

———. *The Vital Issues in the Industrial Conference at Washington, D.C., October 6–23, 1919.* (Pamphlet.)

———. *Works Councils in the United States.* (Research Report No. 21.) Boston: National Industrial Conference Board, 1919.

Slichter, Sumner H. "The Current Labor Policies of American Industries," *Quarterly Journal of Economics,* May 1929, pp. 393–435.

Taylor, Albion G. *Labor Policies of the National Association of Manufacturers.* (University of Illinois Studies in the Social Sciences, Vol. 15, No. 1.) Urbana: University of Illinois, 1928.

U.S., Department of Labor. *Proceedings of the First Industrial Conference, October 6–23, 1919.* Washington, D.C.: Government Printing Office, 1920.

Zimand, Savel. *The Open Shop Drive: Who Is behind It and Where Is It Going?* New York: Bureau of Industrial Research, 1921.

6. *Specific Experiments in Union-Management Cooperation*

The B. and O. Plan

American Federation of Labor. *Railroad Labor Conference, January 19–20, 1929.* 1929. (Pamphlet.)

Beyer, Otto S. "The Technique of Cooperation," *Bulletin of the Taylor Society,* Feb. 1926, pp. 7–20.

———, and Jewell, Bert. *Union Management Cooperation.* 1925. (Pamphlet.)

Federated Shop Crafts, Railway Employes' Department. *The Cooperative Policy of the Railway Employes' Department.* 1926. (Pamphlet.)

Jewell, Bert. "Labor's Appraisal of Principles, Methods and Results," *Bulletin of the Taylor Society,* Feb. 1926, pp. 21–26.

Thornton, Henry W. "Management's Appraisal of Principles, Methods and Results," *Bulletin of the Taylor Society,* Feb. 1926, pp. 26–29.

Willard, Daniel. *The Baltimore and Ohio Railroad Company's Labor Relations.* 1924. (Pamphlet.)

Wolf, H. D. *The Railroad Labor Board.* Chicago: University of Chicago Press, 1927.

Wood, Louis A. *Union-Management Cooperation on the Railroads.* New Haven: Yale University Press, 1931.

The Clothing Unions

Budish, J. M., and Soule, George. *The New Unionism in the Clothing Industry.* New York: Harcourt Brace, 1920.

Haas, Francis J. *Shop Collective Bargaining.* Washington, D.C.: Catholic University of America, 1922.

Haber, W. G. "Workers' Rights and the Introduction of Machinery in the Men's Clothing Industry," *Journal of Political Economy,* August 1925, pp. 388–409.

Hillman, Sidney. "The Problem of Employment in the Clothing Industries," *Advance,* August 5, 19, 26, 1927.

Levine, Louis. *The Women's Garment Workers.* New York: Huebsch, 1924.

Palmer, Gladys L. "Job-Conscious Unionism in the Chicago Men's Clothing Industry," *American Economic Review,* March 1930, pp. 28–36.

U.S., Department of Labor. *Wages and Hours of Labor in the Men's Clothing Industry: 1911–1930.* (Bulletin of Bureau of Labor Statistics No. 503.) Washington, D.C.: Government Printing Office, 1931.

Wolman, Leo. *The Clothing Workers of Chicago.* Chicago: Chicago Joint Board, Amalgamated Clothing Workers, 1922.

The Textile Unions

"The Coming of Industry to the South," *Annals of the American Academy of Political and Social Science,* 153 (Jan. 1931).

Dunn, Robert W., and Hardy, Jack. *Labor and Textiles.* New York: International Publishers, 1931.

Information Service, Federal Council of Churches of Christ in America. *Industrial Relations in a Hosiery Mill.* May 19, 1928.

Mitchell, Broadus, and Mitchell, George Sinclair. *The Industrial Revolution in the South.* Baltimore: Johns Hopkins University Press, 1930.

Mitchell, George Sinclair. *Textile Unionism and the South.* Chapel Hill: University of North Carolina Press, 1931.

Smith, J. F., O'Connell, J. P., and Goodell, F. "Naumkeag Experiment," *Bulletin of the Taylor Society,* April 1930, pp. 63–79.

Taylor, George. *The Full-Fashioned Hosiery Worker: His Changing Economic Status.* Philadelphia: University of Pennsylvania Press, 1931.

———. *Significant Post-War Changes in the Full-Fashioned Hosiery Industry.* Philadelphia: University of Pennsylvania Press, 1929.

Index

INDEX

www.ingramcontent.com/pod-product-compliance
Ingram Content Group UK Ltd.
Pitfield, Milton Keynes, MK11 3LW, UK
UKHW020208290926
15470UKWH00001B/68

9 780837 163758